DEAR GARY
    MERRY CHRIS̶t̶
BLESSED   NEW
BOOK   BE   AS   M̶
INSPIRATION   TO   Y̶   WAS
TO   ME.   ENJOY   GOD   BLESS!
        RIAN

                    - DUBAI 2008 -

Kent Rymate

This book is simple, yet profound. It will speak to you no matter where you are in your Christian walk. My friend Kent speaks out of years of pastoral teaching and leadership, so the note of experiential authenticity is present. The personal experiences he shares affirm his teaching and provide a down-to-earth reality missing from too many Christian books, so count on being challenged and changed. You'll be glad this winsome witness has come to you.

—MAXIE DUNNAM
Chancellor, Asbury Theological Seminary

"What is God's will for my life?" Most everyone asks this question. In this practical, insightful book, Kent Reynolds draws upon biblical revelation and personal experience gained through many years of pastoral ministry to address this vitally important issue. Read it and enjoy the journey God has for you.

—ROBERT WHITLOW
Best-selling author of *The List*

For several years now I've been listening to Kent Reynolds (his secretary is kind enough to send me his sermons on CD). I personally believe he is one of the strongest preachers in America. So, quite naturally, I was curious to see if he could express himself in book form as well. I was not disappointed. The man writes well. His no-nonsense style gets to the point and brings you along with him. You will use this book and recommend it to your friends. It captures the heart of that perennial question, "What next?" It gives us invaluable insight as to how we can best listen, and then hear from God. I believe that you will be well on the way to the answer to that question before you finish the final chapter.

—ROBERT G. TUTTLE, JR.
Professor of World Christianity
Asbury Theological Seminary

The Will of God is a powerful book for developing your ability to discern and walk in God's purposes for your life. It speaks to a wide audience and can be applied to all cultural settings.

—BISHOP BARNABAS MTOKAMBALI
Tanzania Assemblies of God

THE WILL OF GOD

THE
WILL OF
GOD

KENT
REYNOLDS

CREATION
HOUSE

THE WILL OF GOD by Kent A. Reynolds
Published by Creation House
A Strang Company
600 Rinehart Road
Lake Mary, Florida 32746
www.creationhouse.com

This book or parts thereof may not be reproduced in any form, stored in a retrieval system, or transmitted in any form by any means—electronic, mechanical, photocopy, recording, or otherwise—without prior written permission of the publisher, except as provided by United States of America copyright law.

Unless otherwise noted, all Scripture quotations are from the Holy Bible, New International Version. Copyright © 1973, 1978, 1984, International Bible Society. Used by permission.

Scripture quotations marked RSV are from the Revised Standard Version of the Bible. Copyright © 1946, 1952, 1971 by the Division of Christian Education of the National Council of the Churches of Christ in the USA. Used by permission.

Scripture quotations marked KJV are from the King James Version of the Bible.

Scripture quotations marked NKJV are from the New King James Version of the Bible. Copyright © 1979, 1980, 1982 by Thomas Nelson, Inc., publishers. Used by permission.

Cover design by Bill Johnson

Copyright © 2008 by Kent A. Reynolds
All rights reserved

Library of Congress Control Number: 2007940830
International Standard Book Number: 978-1-59979-310-8

First Edition

08 09 10 11 12 — 9 8 7 6 5 4 3 2 1
Printed in the United States of America

This book is dedicated to
Sandy Timnick Reynolds.

CONTENTS

INTRODUCTION

How can I know the will of God for my life? How can I hear from God? These are the two questions people have most frequently asked me in my pastoral ministry of over thirty years. To help answer these questions, I have written this book.

If you are a son or daughter of God through Jesus Christ, not only *can* you hear from God but you *should* hear from God. It is the birthright our heavenly Father has given every one of His children. I have found that God does not necessarily tell us His will in some all-encompassing pronouncement about the course of our lives. Yes, God will tell us some specific things we need to know, but we will find that His will unfolds moment by moment as we learn to walk in the counsel of His guidance. That is what this book is all about.

As a pastor, I have often faced the interesting challenge of teaching important spiritual and biblical principles to groups of people which included both those who had never heard the gospel and mature believers who had been walking with Christ for years. At these times, the Spirit of God has somehow been able use the same teaching to speak to each person at the place of their own individual need and understanding. As I began writing this book, I wanted to allow the Spirit to do the same thing.

As I wrote this book, my desire was to speak to those who are just beginning their journey of faith and are unsure of how to establish a lasting and fulfilling relationship with God. If you want to give this book to a new believer or someone who wants to know more about the Christian faith, I believe it will be very helpful to them. At the same time, I believe that those who are seeking a deeper and more profound walk with God will benefit from the insights expressed here. My desire and prayer is that reading this will help mature believers grow closer to God and be more effective in their spiritual life.

This book will take us through the process of making sure that we are truly converted—that all of who we are has been brought into and under the blessing and authority of God. This is the first and most important first step. I will talk about the place of the Bible in forming our perspective and shaping the way we think. I will lay the foundation for developing spiritual discernment—the ability to see and evaluate things from God's perspective. We will consider the vital role of the Holy Spirit and His profound work of both revealing and releasing the will of God for us. We will talk about what it means to be led by the Lord and how that works in the lives of believers.

I will teach the importance of practicing the fundamentals of the faith. We will look at priorities and what is most important to us as we live. I will warn about some pitfalls and fallacies, as well as some obstacles we face. We will look at the importance of worship, the importance of which I too often neglected in my own walk. I have come to realize how vital it is in both understanding and walking in the will of God. Finally, we will each have an opportunity to examine our own destiny in Christ through the unfolding of God's purposes for our lives.

As you read this book, the deep desire and prayer of my heart is that you will be met with the reality of God and encounter the One who loves you more than you can possibly imagine.

Chapter 1

INTRODUCED AT CONVERSION

EARLY ONE MONDAY morning I was alone in my office at the United Methodist church where I had served as pastor for several years. I often enjoyed the quiet early morning before anyone else was there because I was able to work without interruption. That morning, however, our custodian, a precious man who had been employed by the church for over thirty years, came to my door. He said that a woman was in the sanctuary and needed to speak to me.

Normally, I do not see women alone unless one of our secretaries is at her desk right outside my office. However, I sensed that I needed to see this woman right away. She was a shy woman who appeared to be in her thirties, and I had never seen her before. If she attended our church, I was not aware of it. She did not appear to be wealthy, but neither did she seem like the many people who were struggling in the depths of poverty that often came by for assistance. She had deep, gentle eyes that reflected a tender heart and an inner strength that arose from depth of character revealed through years of struggle.

We sat down in chairs in front of my desk, and she immediately asked if I could share one or two scriptures to help her through the difficulties she was facing. "Well," I said, hoping to lighten the mood without being flippant, "there are a lot of verses in the Bible. Why not tell me what's going on?"

She began what is an all-too-common litany of hardship. A near lethal combination of things had been thrust upon her against her will, along with many poor choices of her own, which had made it worse. As is so often the case, it involved a man, a marriage, and children. Nothing was working, and her methods of coping were wearing thin.

As she spoke, I sensed a resonant spirituality in her, an obvious awareness of faith. She told me that she prayed often, and from her initial request I saw that she had a basic reverence for the Bible. She had a foundational knowledge of God, and some measure of moral understanding. However, as we proceeded, it became clear that she did not know Jesus Christ, His personal love for her, and the possibility of new life in His name.

I began to tell her that all the scriptures she had so often read pointed to Jesus Christ. Opening the Bible to Ephesians 1:3–8, I directed her attention to the words which depict the glorious "riches of God's grace that he lavished on us" in Christ (Eph. 1:7–8). These verses are laced with references to the fact that God has done all things through and for His Son. They have a cadence—"in Christ" (Eph. 1:3), "in him" (Eph. 1:4), "through Jesus Christ" (Eph. 1:5), "in the One he loves" (Eph. 1:6)—that undeniably points to Jesus Christ as the source of everything in God. Absolutely everything is for and about Jesus.

As the Holy Spirit began to do His marvelous work in her heart, it was as if someone had suddenly turned on the light in a dark room in which she had stumbled about for years. Everything that had always been there, hidden from her eyes, now came to life. "Oh! Oh!" she cried, "There He is! Oh, yes! There He is again!"

She literally began pawing at the page, and I no longer had to point her to Jesus. She was seeing Him with her own eyes. She saw Him in the words she was reading and sensed Him in her heart as the Spirit gave glory to the beloved Son of God. It was as if the Spirit of the living God was bringing to life all the dormant scripture she had piled up in her heart throughout the years. The Word of God began to come so alive in her heart that I thought she might explode.

It was therefore easy and quite natural for me to invite her to kneel right there in front of my desk. As I guided her in a prayer of repentance and surrender, she beautifully acknowledged the lordship of Jesus Christ and received His love and forgiveness. I was privileged beyond measure to watch her be born again in a moment marked by such glorious wonder that nothing can compare to it. When she returned to her seat, there was something brand new about her. It was clear that God had not simply put a Band-Aid on her troubles. Something quite significant had occurred in her life.

Like this precious woman who had read the Bible and even prayed for years, many people have difficulty discerning the will of God largely because they have never been truly converted. Conversion is the process of bringing one's entire being under the authority of God and to be immersed in God's life. It is a process. This kind of conversion does not happen overnight, but it has important high water marks along the way. And like every process, it has a beginning.

A Change of Authority

I wish I could say that everything in this woman's life miraculously turned around in an instant, but that would be overselling the moment. There was, however, a significant change of the authority that governed her life, and the importance of this cannot be overstated.

Authority is a major issue in life, and it affects everything about us. First, we must realize that we have authority over our own lives, and we can yield it to whomever and whatever we choose. If we yield ourselves to that which is good, there will be positive effects. Conversely, if we yield ourselves to that which is bad, the effects will naturally be detrimental. We are all under authority of some kind, be it professional, familial, or religious. This is necessary and good if the authority under which we function is healthy, just, and benevolent.

Some of the most difficult people to deal with are those who have authority issues and claim to be under no one's authority at all. Such people are often critical of every authority and find fault with every boss, pastor, parent, or teacher. They may try to assert that they are their own master and are yielded to no one. Yet, they fail to realize that they have made *self* their master, and *self* can be quite the tyrant.

The process of conversion begins when we give God permission to work in our lives. Many of us beg God to work in our lives but do not give God the right to do so. When we do, we may not feel it or realize it cognitively, but the change is very real. When we yield to the lordship of Jesus Christ, we have willingly exchanged the rule of *self* in our lives for the loving dominion of Christ.

When we do this, we may not even be aware of how monumental it is. When we say, "Lord Jesus, my life is no longer my own, but Yours," we have not only given Him authority to work in us, but we have also given Him permission to guide and direct us. Jesus therefore has authority *in* our lives and has responsibility *for* our lives. It is a responsibility that is parental in nature, and the Lord takes it very seriously. This is why the Bible says that if we receive Christ and believe in His name He gives us "the right to become children of God" (John 1:12). There is a huge difference between working *for* God as a hireling and working *with* God as a son or daughter. To willingly yield to Christ's authority opens our lives to the fullness of His blessing.

Yielding to the lordship of Jesus Christ does not mean that we abdicate our responsibility for decision-making. It would be nice if we could simply sit back and allow God to make our decisions for us, but He will not do this. As God's life is formed within us and as our minds become more attuned to God's council, then our thinking and our decisions will be based more and more on God's leading. We do not do this alone. By yielding, we say that our lives belong to God. The ultimate authority and responsibility for the direction and welfare of our lives is in the hands of the God who created us and loves us.

More Than Assumed Christianity

One of the challenges of contemporary Christianity is the widely-held assumption that someone is converted simply because they go to church or know some of the language of the faith. However, many people who claim to be Christians are still effectively in charge of their own lives. They—not God—are calling the shots.

We cannot ignore the reality that many church pews are full of people who assume their Christianity by matriculation. They were christened as infants, trained as confirmands, have been fairly regular in their church attendance, and thus assume their salvation because they did everything their church told them to do. Yet, they have never really received Christ as Savior or given Him authority in their lives.

Many faithful, loving, praying folks who believe in God have never entered into an "I hereby declare" moment in which they crown Jesus Christ as the supreme authority of their lives. Much like the woman who came to my office that day, they read the Bible and pray, but have never given permission for Jesus Christ to exercise His loving dominion. Things often change dramatically when they do.

This is what happened to Bill, a life-long faithful church member who was part of a short-term missionary team I led to Mexico several years ago. As our team was eating breakfast with some of the local people, Bill found himself sitting alone with a precious Mexican evangelist named Patricio. Bill spoke no Spanish, Patricio spoke little English. Somehow he managed to ask Bill when he had become a Christian. Bill explained that his parents were faithful to church and had taken him to church throughout his childhood. He added that he had remained faithful to the church all his adult life as well.

Patricio did not understand Bill's response. He actually thought Bill had misunderstood his question. In broken English he said, "I did not ask you about church, I asked you when you became a Christian." Because it was said so totally without condemnation or personal agenda, it pierced Bill's heart. That night, after we had worked on the construction of a church building for a congregation in that little Mexican village, we shared a time of joyful worship to God. After I preached and gave an invitation for salvation, many of the Mexican people came forward. But the first one to come was Bill.

With tears in his eyes and the glory of God on his face, Bill received the life of God that the Bible has promised. He gave God the best thing he could give Him: His life. Bill was certainly a good and loving man before then, but something changed for him that night. In fact, many things changed. Sure, he was still loving and good. But a new spiritual authority and understanding had begun to function within him. His walk with the Lord was deeper, richer, and more personal. And God's sense of calling on His life was never more profound.

Not long after we returned home, I saw him at church one day, fixing something as he always did. "It's all different now, isn't it?" I said.

"Yes," he smiled, "it certainly is."

Imagine for a moment that a young man is pretending to be in the army. He wears military-style clothing, uses military-type jargon, struts around in presumed military fashion, carries an imaginary weapon, and generally acts as if he were in the army. There is just one problem: he is not in the army.

He has not enlisted, signed the contract, taken the oath of induction, nor committed his life to the military. In short, he is a military wannabe. On the other hand, imagine someone who did, in fact, join the army but was never committed to it, never did the drills, refused to use the language or wear the uniform, submit to military authority, or participate in any of the activities that define a soldier. He is a fake.

So it is with the Christian life. We have to join. We must at some level "sign the contract," take the oath of induction, and formally commit our lives to the way of Christ. Once we have enlisted for service in the Lord's army, we can expect to receive information from our High Command. And we need to live as if we belong in His army by actively developing a life of devotion, discipline, service, and relationship.

When the children of Israel went into Canaan, God told them that they were not to take the land "all at once" (Deut. 7:22). Bit by bit, foot by foot, they were to conquer the land until all of it was subdued. Similarly, we are not converted all at once, but in stages and levels, "from one degree of glory to another" (2 Cor. 3:18, RSV). Please remember that you are not being converted to Christianity but to Christ. Your task is not to assume new religious rules but to begin to walk in a new way of life—Christ's way.

In the moment of decision, a person fully becomes a child of God with all of the benefits of the atoning work of the Cross and the immortality of what the Bible calls everlasting life. Then begins the process of bringing every area of life into submission to the will of God: one's heart, one's thinking, one's worldview, one's relationships, one's ambitions, one's body, one's possessions, one's work, one's family, and one's future. It is a process that will include many significant moments of advance and occasional setbacks.

Conversion is an event, a series of events, and a process. It is an event in that there should be some discernable moment when the love of God touches your life and you willingly respond. It is a series of events in that there might be many significant moments of challenge, growth, hardship, and victory. These moments contribute to an overall process which will hopefully move you to a deeper understanding of God's goodness and purpose and bring more of your life into the flow of God's blessing. For most people, some of the most difficult challenges in the process of conversion are releasing one's body to the Lord, surrendering one's finances to the Lord, and relinquishing one's future to the Lord. I find that I need to continually surrender more and more of my life and my will to the sovereignty of God. Each moment of surrender is vital in establishing and maintaining a healthy and effective relationship with God.

From Death to Life

The Bible tells us that we are always saved *from* something, and *to* something else. The Israelites were saved from Egypt, to the Promised Land—from slavery to freedom. In Christ, we are transformed from darkness to light, from death to life. God's desire is not simply to rescue us from the dominion of self-centered living. He wants to transform us to new life— new direction, new perspective on people and the world, new purpose, new joy, and a new power source for living. New life refers to Christ Himself living in us and giving us access to His power, discernment, and wisdom.

Many people get the *from* part right, but they so often fail to embrace the *to* part. They are caught in a virtual limbo between Egypt and the Promised Land. They may not be sinning anymore, but they are certainly not walking in new life. There is a huge difference between being a reformed sinner and "a new creation" (2 Cor. 5:17).

When the apostle Paul began to travel into the area of what is now primarily Turkey and Greece, he encountered people who were quite fatalistic about life. They believed that certain unknown factors determined where and into what social class they were born. In their understanding, things were the way they were, and they could do nothing to change their fate. Imagine how strange Paul seemed to them when he came with a message of hope—that nothing was set in stone, and everyone, whether rich or poor, of common or noble birth, could have a whole new life by the power of the One true and living God.

How sad it is that many people continue to have a fatalistic view of life today! They adhere to the philosophy that their situation is just the way it is and cannot be changed. However, the gospel of Jesus Christ is the *good news* that the course of one's life is not predetermined. Anyone can have a new life by trusting in Christ. If the death of Christ brings forgiveness of sins and reconciliation with God, "How much more, having been reconciled, shall we be saved through his life?" (Rom. 5:10). If we, through baptism, enter into the death of Christ, we also enter into His resurrection and "live a new life" (Rom. 6:4).

Genesis, Again

When Jesus rose from the dead, He became the prototype of a whole new species of human beings. He is, as 1 Corinthians 15:45 identifies Him, "the last Adam." The first Adam was the firstborn of the original creation. He obviously became flawed, and all who descended from him—all of us—share the same flawed human nature. Jesus was the firstborn of a whole new race of human beings (Col. 1:18). In Him, God began the regeneration of the whole earth, a process He started with human beings and one that will eventually encompass the entire created order. Jesus came to bring a new way of life for a new humanity.

On two occasions the Bible uses the word *regeneration*. It occurs in the Book of Titus 3:5. It is translated from a Greek word, *paliggenesiva*, which literally means to be recreated as in new birth. So when the Bible speaks of regeneration it is as if God is performing a "new Genesis." God is in the process of regenerating or recreating the whole earth and restoring it to the original perfection it once enjoyed. Creation knows this even better than we do. Romans 8:19–22 tells us that all creation is groaning in travail, awaiting the dawning of the new day when it will be restored. Isaiah 55:12 describes that day as a time when creation will be so overjoyed that the mountains and the hills will break forth in singing and the "trees of the field will clap their hands."

Creation will no longer be subject to disease, decay, and death. Predatory activity will cease, and one species will no longer fear another. Isaiah 11:6-8 prophesies that the wolf will dwell with the lamb; the leopard will lie down with the kid; the calf and the lion together; and a little child will be able to play over the hole of a poisonous snake.

Human beings are included in this process. The term *born again* is not some religious catchphrase, but it describes a person who has entered into the process of new creation. We were born the first time of a flawed human species. We gave no personal consent to it. Now, however, we can choose to be part of God's new creation—His "new Genesis"—through Christ. We can be born again, not of imperfect, human seed, but of God, never to be subject to death again.

Conversion is much more than simply fine-tuning an old model. True conversion is crossing the line and transferring the authority of our lives from the reign of self to the dominion of God. It is giving God permission to work in us until all of our heart, soul, mind, and strength are brought into submission to His will, to participate in His new creation. The process of conversion begins by yielding to the will of God.

The point is quite simple. We cannot expect to discern the will of God if we are not converted. We cannot know the will of God if we are still living life on our own terms and expecting God to conform to our expectations.

Chapter 2

SUBMITTING TO
THE WORD OF GOD

I F WE ARE going to discern the will of God, the Bible must have a prominent place in our lives. The Holy Scriptures have been and continue to be the primary means of communication between God and humanity. As we immerse ourselves in the Word of God, we will find that it is one of the foremost means by which God shapes our thinking, our character, and our behavior. The Word works in conjunction with the Spirit of God. Together they give insight and understanding into the will of God and work in the formation of our nature. Through this process, God's will and purpose are formed within us and released through us.

The Bible is quite controversial these days. Many find it difficult to understand, and some object to the way it has been used, or misused, to justify heinous acts and the condemnation of certain people. Many are concerned about the origins of the Bible, how it has been translated over the years, and even the process by which certain books have been included or excluded during the process of its canonization.

These are legitimate concerns and challenging issues. Nonetheless, God has spoken through His Word throughout history, and He continues to speak each time we open it. The fact that some people misuse the Bible grieves me deeply. However, this does not keep me from believing its revelation and power any more than seeing people overeat keeps me from enjoying food. The testimony of countless faithful witnesses throughout the centuries points to the power and authority of the Bible, and it has had the most profound impact on my life as well.

I grew up in a good home but we didn't read the Bible or talk much about God. We went to church fairly regularly, but we were not particularly active in any of those we attended. I had an awareness of God from an early age, but for the most part did not live as one who was aware of His reality. It is difficult for me to understand how I could have claimed an awareness of God but actually lived in ways which were the opposite of everything God represents. It would be years later, as God began calling me to the pastoral ministry that I began to make serious attempts to bring my life in line with God's will. It was a long process for me. God was patient and loved me even when I did not deserve it. The role which the Bible would play in the process of my own conversion cannot be overstated. Still today, it is the primary source of my understanding of the nature and will of God.

When I was in seminary, I studied the Bible extensively, mainly as an academic exercise. What I learned there has helped me to understand the process by which the Bible can be more properly interpreted. It gave me principles of sound interpretation which, if implemented wisely, can keep us from interpreting Scripture erroneously to suit our own selfish desires. However, true faith in Scripture takes more than an academic understanding.

It was not until the early days of my pastoral ministry that I really began reading the Bible in earnest. When I first started in ministry, I was the pastor of a small church near Atlanta, Georgia. Each morning, I would read from a Bible—the King James Version—that the Gideons had placed in a hotel somewhere. I cannot explain to you how or why it deeply resonated with me. Somehow, I knew it was truth, and I believed it. I heard God's voice in my soul as I read, and I still do today. I attribute my faith in the Bible to the pure grace of God, who gave me faith to believe what He has said.

No, I did not understand all of Bible, and I cannot claim to understand all of it today. Learning from the Bible is a process we never complete. It is an ever-unfolding revelation of the depth of God's heart and purposes. Back then, I did not live according to the Bible as I should have, and today I am still trying to bring more of my life in line with its precepts. But in the depths of my soul, I knew—and know—that God's Word was truth and it is a profound source of God's life.

It took some time before I added prayer to my morning ritual, and it took even longer for the truth of Scripture to begin to show up in the way I lived. However, I like to think that in those early morning hours, God was beginning to write His Word on my heart. I fell in love with the Bible. Yes, it is sometimes very convicting as it cuts across the grain of my thoughts or my actions. Yet, it is a fundamental source of God's life, the primary way He speaks to you and me. Every other expression of God will always be consistent with His written Word.

Many people struggle to believe the Bible, and this can be a difficult hurdle to cross. It is nevertheless true that we cannot circumvent the authority of Scripture if we are going to walk with God according to His will. Never confuse people's interpretation of the Bible with the Bible itself. Teachers can help unlock its precepts but there is no substitute for each of us drinking from that well of God's life! I have come to realize that time with God and His Word is critical to our walk of faith. The history recorded in the Bible is intriguing and the stories are often passionate. However, Scripture is infinitely more than history or entertainment, insightful writing or inspiring prose. Regardless of its literary form or the way it has been interpreted and acted out by others, the Bible is the truth of God.

Changing the Way We Think

The Bible is one of the primary means by which God transforms our thinking, our behavior, and our very nature. It has a transcendent power greater than words printed on the pages. God created the world by His word (Heb. 11:3). By the word of the Lord, people are born again (Rom. 10:17). By the Word of the Lord, lives are changed, people are healed, situations are altered, and doors are opened. Try to stop seeing the Bible as an antiquated text and begin to see it as an incredible source of life.

As we open ourselves to receive the ministry of Scripture and immerse ourselves in its truth, we can begin to experience what it means to be formed by the Word of God. One of the first important steps for me came as I began to read the Psalms. It is a good place to start. I was often astounded as I saw my own heart's cry there on the pages. It became an important vehicle of personal relevance for me, the initial place of personal connection. From that point, I began to sense that God really did know me and care about me. More and more, I began to see my own life connect with the Scriptures. I began to see certain principles which made sense to me. And I began to sense God's presence more and more as I read each day.

The Bible is not simply a religious icon, but a means by which God imparts His life to us. It not only gives information for the mind, but it also has the power to transform our thinking, our nature, and our behavior to be more like Christ, the living Word of God. The process begins with a change of heart, but it also produces a profound change in the way we think.

One of my concerns as a pastor has been the fact that many of the people who sit in church pews week after week often think similarly as those outside the church. Many Christians have the same prejudices, angst, greed, fear, and anger as those who do not even profess to know God. This is a major problem. Doesn't it naturally follow that someone who is under the influence of a wise and loving God would think differently (let alone live differently) than someone who is not?

I do not intend to imply that those who walk with Christ all think the same way. There is great diversity in the kingdom of God. However, we cannot expect to function in the will of God if we are still thinking in a carnal fashion. We often talk about Christ producing a change of *heart*, but He also brings about a change of *mind*. I am not trying to assert that those of us who profess Christ are somehow superior to others. I am simply trying to make the point that God's influence on our lives should have significant effects on the way we think.

The unredeemed mind cannot fathom the mysteries of the Spirit of God. In fact, spiritual reality is foolishness to the unspiritual mind (1 Cor. 2:14). Dr. Martin Luther King Jr. once said, "The heart cannot be right if the head is totally wrong"[1] Conversion of the heart is not enough to bring us in line with the will of God. There has to be a conversion of the intellect as well.

For instance, it is possible for a person to be one who is determined to refute every biblical precept. I have seen this many times. Such a person is not someone on an honest journey to find a meaningful basis for living their lives. This type of person is a committed skeptic. He or she can do a perpetual intellectual dance and find fault with every scriptural precept. If you are this kind of person, the life of faith will be a most difficult journey. You can, if you are determined, keep truth at arm's length. I actually believe that keeping truth at arm's length is often a means to keep commitment at arm's length as well. If you don't believe the Bible is truth, you do not have to yield to it, commit to it, or live it.

Many people say we should not leave our brains at the door when it comes to matters of faith. I could not agree more. How foolish to assert that faith implies an absence of sound thinking. No one should advocate mindless religion. But neither can we expect to go very far with God with an intellect that is unrelenting in its skepticism and carnality. Our intellectual abilities are a gift from God—not to be denied in our life of faith and not to be exploited for our selfish benefit. It is in humbly submitting the gift of our mind to the Lord that He releases that precious gift in its true purpose. A mind that is properly submitted to the One who created it is a powerful tool for good in the world.

The redeemed mind, bathed in the power of the Spirit and transformed by the renewal of the Word, can begin to understand and appropriate wisdom from on high. While it is true that faith involves believing in things that are unseen and virtually un-provable, it is not mindless and irrational. It is not blind acceptance of the unknown. We cannot have faith in something we neither know nor understand. On the contrary, faith is the assurance of what we know to be true about God.

We cannot trust in something unknown. We cannot just create some god in our minds to explain things we do not understand and give meaning to life. Faith functions in the context of our relationship with God, His revelation in Christ, and our experience of His reality. We put our trust in a God we have come to know and are coming to know more every day. Our human intelligence can never reason its way to God, and we cannot presume to figure it all out. Yet, because faith is not simply a matter of feeling and intuition, brainpower has a significant role in it.

The ways of God are not random, senseless, or irrational. They are not built upon mindless, shallow spirituality, but they reflect the consistent intelligence of His design. No human being can completely fathom God's precepts, but neither is His wisdom hidden. God's ways and will do make sense once we begin to understand the principles by which spiritual wisdom and understanding operate. As intelligent beings, we can begin to grasp His wisdom and truth, while seeking to live and communicate it.

Many people unfortunately have a life philosophy that is an amalgamation of misquoted Bible verses, simplistic proverbs, a dash of so-called common sense, and some outrageous ideas. Culture, family, and experience all combine to color how we see ourselves and others, how we view the world, and how we develop our dreams and ambitions.

Unfortunately, there may be a lot of brokenness in the way we think. Negative life experiences may distort reality or cause us to see things through the debilitating influences of the wounds we have suffered. One of the hard lessons I have had to learn is that I sometimes have a flawed view of things. Because of this, God's loving transformation includes changes in our often-distorted thinking.

It is actually possible to begin to understand some of God's ways as we read the Bible and immerse ourselves in its truth. If we do not lose heart and continue seeking God, Scripture will come alive to us—in more ways than simply knowing biblical facts and figures. We can begin to understand, in some small measure, how God thinks, how He works, and what His plans are. We will even begin to understand more about who we are and how we fit into those plans. Our identity is intrinsically tied to the nature and purposes of God, our loving Creator. As we come to know more fully the counsel of God, we will see how His plans for our individual lives always fit into His desires for all humankind.

As we read the Bible regularly, we should at some point try to read all of it. But you don't have to begin that way. Start in the Psalms or maybe one of the Gospels. One of the things I have found to be helpful is to select a scripture passage that speaks to me and read it every day, perhaps for a few weeks. As I "live" with this scripture and think about it in my daily routine, I have often found that God might shed light on it through certain experiences in my daily life. As time passes, the scriptures we live with will begin to shape how we see things. God's Word will begin to form who we are.

Can you see how the Word can come alive and shape your character and nature in accordance with the will of God? We can begin to think like God thinks, see the world through God's eyes, build our dreams and ambitions on God's desires, and see others with God's heart. Discerning the will of God is infinitely more than simply receiving information or direction from God!

Revealing God's Rightful Place

The book of Genesis tells us that Adam and Eve, the first human beings, lived in the Garden of Eden. They had everything they needed in the original pristine beauty of the earth. Because they were originally created immortal, they had no fear of death. They were given dominion over the earth and everything that lived in it. This does not mean that they could brutishly rule over it, nor squander its resources on selfish living. The earth still belonged to God. As Psalm 24:1 says, "The earth is the Lord's and everything in it."

When the Bible says that God gave dominion to human beings, it is telling us that God entrusted Adam and Eve with the sacred stewardship of the earth. He gave men and women—the crowning glory of His creation—a caretaker's authority and responsibility to tend and subdue the earth in accordance with the will of God. They were to work not as hirelings—slavishly toiling for their living—but as His children who would one day inherit it all. God's intent was to

— 21 —

share the wonders of the earth with sons and daughters who would lovingly care for it. Ideally, they would cherish their inheritance and work hard to maintain, protect, and multiply what would one day be theirs. They had a vested interest in taking good care of it.

Adam and Eve were given only one rule in the Garden of Eden: God would maintain His rightful place and determine what was good and what was evil. This was symbolically represented in what was called the "tree of the knowledge of good and evil" (Gen. 2:9). God, who created all things, was the One who would ultimately determine what was right and wrong, moral and immoral, good and evil. Because of this, He occupied His rightful place as the center of all life. Thus the tree of the knowledge of good and evil was placed in the center of the garden. By looking to God as the center and source of all life, Adam and Eve were to be God-centered and look to Him as the source of right and wrong. Unfortunately, the greatest problems of life occur when others try to usurp God's rightful place and exalt themselves in God's place.

Something of an evil nature—malicious, intentional, and calculating—came on the scene. It originated with Lucifer, a jealous, vain angelic being in the heavenly court of almighty God. Lucifer wanted to rule in the place of God and led about a third of the angels in a great insurrection against Him and His sovereign authority. The battle for supremacy moved from heaven to earth. Lucifer, who is also called the devil, has always resented the rule of God. He is angry and bitter that he himself could not reign in God's place. This has caused him to hate God, the ways of God, and especially God's children. His aim is to pollute God's kingdom and undermine God's authority in any way he can. Because his primary intent is to exalt himself to the place of God, the devil tries to establish his authority over everything on the earth, especially over human beings, the crowning glory of God's creation and the primary recipients of God's love.

This enemy of God began his assault on God's children at the very beginning. It was not a direct confrontation, but it was much more subtle and insidious. Wiley and dangerous as a snake, Satan asked Eve, "Did God say that you could not eat of any of the trees of the garden? Are you *sure* God said that? Are you quite certain it was the tree of the knowledge of good and evil? Could it have perhaps been another tree? Perhaps you are mistaken, or you misunderstood." A confused Eve replied, "Yes, here in Eden we look to God to tell us what is good and what is evil. He gave a grave warning that if we eat the tree in the middle of the garden or even touch it [her addition], we will surely die" (Gen. 3:1–3, author's paraphrase).

"Oh, you won't die," Satan lied. "For God knows that when you eat of it…you will be like God, knowing good from evil" (Gen. 3:5, author's paraphrase). The enticement to be like God and to rule in His place was strong. (It remains so to this day.) It was as though Satan were saying, "You have a brain, don't you Eve? Didn't God give you a brain? Use it! You don't need God telling you right from wrong. Use that brain and decide for yourself. *You can be god of your own life!* "

The fruit had a sensuous, alluring appeal, and it was a delight to her eyes. It could make her strong, independent, wise. Eve bought the lie. Don't blame Eve. She represents all of us! We all buy the lie whenever we believe we don't need God. It's not so much that we don't believe in God or acknowledge His love for us. The independence we seek is a counterfeit for true freedom. We simply want to be in God's place and decide right and wrong for ourselves.

As the human race fell from God's perfect order, we stopped looking to God and started looking to ourselves. In a vain attempt to gain what we perceived to be freedom, we forfeited a God-centered existence for a self-centered one. We didn't know that we were bringing ourselves under the dominion of self, a dictatorial tyrant that makes us obey all its whims and feed its insatiable needs. Our unredeemed human nature is subject to self-centered living and self-centered thinking.

Judges 21:25, one of the most chilling Bible verses, concisely and clearly portrays the human condition after the days of Eden: "In those days, there was no king in Israel; every one did what was right in his own eyes" (NKJV). In other words, human beings, left to themselves, will always choose what arises out of their own self will.

The redeeming work of God is to return us to the place where we give up a self-centered existence for a God-centered one. We can no longer sit on the throne as if we are the god of our lives, but we must return God to His rightful place. Only then are can we expect to walk in His will.

Our Ultimate Authority for Truth

The Bible is more than an expression of God's mind, will, or the things He has said and done. It is an expression of who He is, and it conveys the fullness of the divine nature. Everything God does is an expression of His nature. Christ is called "the Word" for this very reason. In the words of John

1:14, "The Word became flesh and made His dwelling among us. We have seen His glory, the glory of the One and Only, who came from the Father, full of grace and truth."

God desires to be known, and His self-revelation is full and complete. Christ emanated from the bosom of the Father, from the very depths of God's very essence (John 1:18, RSV). Colossians 1:19 teaches, "For God was pleased to have all his fullness dwell in [Christ]." Because Christ is so much the fullness of God, Jesus declared in John 14:9, "Anyone who has seen me has seen the Father."

Creation itself is an expression of the nature of God. The vastness of the heavens, the movement of the seasons, the patterns and make-up of the natural order all give insight into who God is. Even the inner working of the human body shows us in some measure about God and even life itself. When Jesus taught about the kingdom of God, He often referred to nature, not just because He was speaking to a largely agrarian society but also because God has woven His reality and truth into the very fabric of creation.

Consider the detail of the world, the intricate beauty of the petals of a rose, the unfathomable mystery of the power contained in the invisible atom, the alignment of the systems of the human body, and the rhythm of the seasons and growth patterns of the earth. Creation declares the incomprehensible majesty of our God. He created human beings in His image. He has gone to such great lengths to say, "This is who I am."

No one has to labor unnecessarily groping about trying to unravel the mystery of the existence of God. Right here before us, in full view, God has revealed his glorious majesty to us. Besides creation itself, God has made himself known in Christ, through Scripture and in the presence of the Holy Spirit. Often, he makes himself known through other people as well.

We all have an ultimate authority for truth, whether we consider it in those terms or not. We either look to God as the ultimate authority for truth, or we look to ourselves. We either live a God-centered life or a self-centered one. Yes, there are times we are a mixture of both. Ultimately, however, one or the other must be supreme. Many people who profess Christianity still set their own minds above Scripture and ultimately depend on their own ideas to determine what is true. They may appreciate the Bible and use it for devotional or inspirational material, but they have not submitted themselves to its authority or come under its protection and provision. To walk in submission to the Word of God is also to open the avenue of its blessing.

Truth, like salvation itself, comes from a source outside ourselves. When Jesus came as the Savior of the world, He came from an external source. He was born within the human race and was fully human, but He came from outside the human race—from God (John 3:31). He was born of divine seed (Luke 1:35). Had He been born of human seed, He would have inherited all the natural fallibility of Adam's race and could not have been the perfect, unblemished sacrifice for sin (Heb. 9:14; 1 Pet. 1:19). This is why it makes perfect sense that Jesus was born of the Spirit through a virgin's womb (Matt. 1:23).

Yes, truth comes from God. It comes from above, "from the Father of lights, with whom there is no variance or shadow of change" (James 1:17). It is formed within us and lives within us, but its source is outside us.

Diversity Under the Authority of God's Word

The two single common denominators which unite all people within the kingdom of God are the lordship of Christ and the authority of Scripture. Yet, not all believers think alike. Being submitted to the Word and the will of God does not create some kind of imposed sameness in the way we think. God is not forming a race of automatons. It is good and rich for us to have expressions of diversity in our understanding of Scripture and the way we appropriate its precepts.

Diversity within the kingdom is a lively and vital part of its zest. It is a helpful check and balance against arrogant presumption. However, it is vitally important that the pillars of biblical understanding are held and affirmed. Some who claim to believe the Bible only submit to it when it conforms to their own predetermined belief. Diversity in the kingdom of God must be fully submitted to the authority of the Lord Jesus as expressed in Scripture and enlightened and empowered by the Spirit.

God did not create all people alike. In fact no two people are exactly alike. One of the joys of life is interacting with people of other cultures. The way other people think, live, worship, and follow God provides a unique, vital contribution that can help us broaden the way we see things. Our ability to enjoy this kind of interaction is an incredible benefit of the modern age. As we work together for the good of others, God is bringing believers together from all over the world to shape one another as we share life together. A wise man once told me, "A Christian with a full stomach thinks differently than one with an empty stomach." For example, God is showing us that the way we think as North American Christians differs from the way people think in other parts of the world, even though we all bow the knee to the same Lord.

Expressions of diversity are not limited to the exchange of ideas with other cultures. They also happen within our own sphere of reference and help us experience wholeness and vitality. We often fall into the trap of believing that the biblical instruction for the church to be of "one mind" or of "one accord" means that we should all think the same. However, if everyone in a church thinks alike, they run the risk of becoming ingrown and cultish.

Being of one mind means, in the words of the apostle Paul, each of us having the same mind as that which was in Christ Jesus (Phil. 2:5). It means having the love of Christ for one another and living a life of humility and selfless service to others. Most importantly, it means that all of us are submitted to the biblical pattern for truth. Diversity under scriptural authority is a must. Otherwise we become grossly slanted and lack wholeness in our vision.

Years ago a dear friend and I were talking about the famous Warner Sallman painting of Jesus entitled "Christ at Heart's Door." It depicts Jesus knocking at the door of a quaint Tudor house. Many people believe this painting shows Jesus knocking at the door of a human heart, wanting to come in to our lives. Because there is no knob on the outside of the door, only you or I can let Him in. My friend, however, saw the painting differently. He explained it as Jesus knocking at the door inviting you and me to come out into the world and follow Him. Once we are outside, we can't turn back, because there is no way to get back in.

My friend is a devout believer, and I trust him because he is fully in love with God and submitted to His authority.

When he shared his perspective, he challenged me to consider something new. We all need people of different perspectives around us, not to argue and hold up progress, but to shape and challenge our thinking. We must not be afraid to think about things in different ways.

Our society as a whole—and the Christian community as well—has grown lazy in its ability to think. The polarization of our society has created so-called liberal and conservative camps that substitute ready-made, bumper-sticker type pronouncements for creative, prayerful, often agonizing consideration of what is right. Those who buy into this simplicity see no need to wrestle with issues and, above all, seek God about what is right. That would be entirely too much work.

In an attempt to reach every person, Christians have begun to substitute fill-in-the-blank, easy to understand spiritual platitudes for teaching that requires people to think. Everything has to be simple, neatly packaged, and easy to understand. As some are quick to point out, Jesus used simple analogies and easy to understand parables to teach. While this may have a degree of truth, it is important to recognize that His stories were designed to motivate people to prayerfully ponder in their hearts and then apply it to their lives. He challenged them to consider what it means to be a neighbor, what it means to serve and worship in ways that are pleasing to God. He confronted them with teaching on how genuine, faithful obedience to God transcends cultural lines and how to avoid religious self-righteousness. It is not easy or simplistic to understand how these precepts are to be applied in real life situations.

Television has had a profound impact not only on how we see life, but also our ability to process information. It basically divides life into thirty-minute segments that include, apart from advertising, only twenty-two actual minutes of programming. Within those twenty-two minutes, a story is wrapped in a neat little package and brought to conclusion. Unfortunately, real life does not work the way television portrays it. It is far more complex and its issues require in-depth examination that cannot be completed in less than half an hour.

Discerning truth involves thought, research, waiting in the presence of the Lord, prayer, and hearing from others. Real truth is not simplistic and does not come easily, but it does come to those who are willing to go deep in their deliberations. Too many of us want to be told what something means rather than think it through ourselves. Simple faith does not imply simplistic thinking.

The Antidote to Deception

When Jesus' disciples asked Him about the end of time and His coming again, the first words in His response were, "Watch out that no one deceives you" (Matt. 24:4). This warning is one of the gravest in the Bible. No one is immune from deception, which by definition means that the one deceived is unaware of it. We all have the ability to delude ourselves, and this is all the more reason to view our lives through the Word of God.

If we are honest with ourselves and with God, if we cast our lives fully into the light of God's truth, we are less susceptible to self-delusion. It is not a perfect antidote but it is an important posture. God wants us to live within a community of believers, hopefully a healthy and godly one, so that the influence of other mature believers will keep us in check. Few things in this world are more dangerous than claiming to know the will of God and giving no thought to what someone else might say about it. We should immediately be very suspicious of any Christian organization that maintains it is the only true church and maintains that its way is the only way.

It is no secret that the Bible has been used as a weapon or as a means of control and manipulation. Bible-reading people have been deluded by their misinterpretations to the point of justifying the Crusades, slavery, colonization, wars, and other acts of violence in God's name. The problem lies not in the Bible itself but with those who misinterpret or misrepresent it. They have neither God's heart nor an understanding of His ways.

For instance, Saul of Tarsus, who later became the apostle Paul and an author of much of the New Testament, actually thought he was doing God a service by persecuting Christians (1 Cor. 15:9; Gal. 1:13–14). The problem was not in the scriptures that motivated his zeal, but his shortsighted understanding of what he was reading. However, God enlightened Saul with a new understanding of Scripture and gave him a new heart. As a result, Saul saw the Bible in a new way. The enlightenment he experienced did not refute Scripture, but brought a more complete understanding to what was already there (Acts 17:2).

This shows how God gives spiritual enlightenment and an ever-expanding revelation of truth. He opens our minds to understand what He has said in His Word. Had the people of Jesus' day understood, they would have seen that the Scriptures spoke profoundly of Christ. Our risen Lord revealed this when He appeared to two men on the road to Emmaus and "interpreted [opened] to them in all the scriptures the things concerning himself" (Luke 24:27, RSV). From there they read the Scriptures under God's enlightenment and understood them in a whole new way.

The process of God's enlightenment and revelation is never-ending. The key is that we always read the Bible with humility—knowing that our understanding is limited—and being careful to recognize how insidious spiritual deception really can be. There are some principles we can maintain with certainty. For example, we can be sure of the love of God, the truth of His Word, the incarnation of the Son of God, atonement through Jesus' death on the cross, the truth of Jesus' resurrection, and the fact that He will come again in glory. But we do not know everything. Nothing is worse than a religious know-it-all.

All of us, believer and unbeliever alike, are capable of gross deception. We all have a tendency to say, "I know it's wrong, but I'll do it anyway." The Bible is an external source of truth that challenges our attitudes and actions. We dare not disregard what it has clearly said. Without God's Word, we are susceptible to the quagmire of our inner thoughts and the temptation to rely solely on feelings. Just because we feel something does not necessarily make it truth. Jesus' solemn warning about deception should keep us in God's Word, on our knees, and under the influence and encouragement of a healthy Christian community.

The Most Powerful Mind

As we read the Bible, we must examine our actions in the light of spiritually enlightened intelligence. The most powerful mind is one that is intellectually gifted and fully submitted to the authority of God. It has the power of the human intellect and has been redeemed by the power of God. It is continuously bathed in His Spirit and reflects Jesus Christ. I call it a great mind on its knees.

However, we must guard against the audacity that can come from purely intellectual enlightenment. This is the mind that looks at the Bible and considers itself intellectually superior both to its authors and its precepts. The people who wrote the Bible might not have been nearly as scientifically advanced as we are in the twenty-first century, but that does not mean they were unintelligent. They certainly knew if someone was blind and then miraculously received their sight. They were quite cognizant if someone was dead and then supernaturally brought back to life.

While I am grateful that modern science has improved our understanding of some things and vastly improved the quality of our physical life, I also believe that it blinds our world to the spiritual realities that govern our universe. We demand answers the Bible was never meant to produce. We often have a skewed approach to the truth of Scripture because we are trying to discern spiritual truth from a purely rational mind-set. This will never work.

People sometimes ask me if I believe the Bible is "literally true." What does that mean? To glean the truth of the Bible requires a framework of knowledge that is fundamentally different than the modern scientific method of empirical evidence. This is dramatically illustrated in Jesus' conversation with a religious man named Nicodemus in John 3. As Jesus explained what it means to see, understand, and appropriate the truth of the kingdom of God, He described the renewal of the mind and soul that comes from the Spirit of God. He called it being born again.

Nicodemus, however, was thinking in purely empirical terms and wondered aloud how a man could enter his mother's womb and go through the process of birth a second time (John 3:4). Clearly, these two men were on totally different platforms. It was as if one were talking about basketball and the other baseball. First Corinthians 2:6 says that we do impart certain wisdom, but it is not the wisdom of this world. The "unspiritual" person cannot fathom the mysteries of God—in fact, "they are foolishness to him" (1 Cor. 2:14).

The Biblical witness is that God's reality can pierce the natural world. This is the whole miracle of the coming of Jesus. The incarnation (becoming human) of Christ has many significant ramifications not the least of which is that the power of God has tangible effects in the concrete reality of our lives. When God told Moses that He was aware of the suffering of the Israelites and had "come down to deliver them" (Exod. 3:7–8), He revealed that He, the Creator of the universe, was aware of Israel's condition and was also going to take action to remedy it. We believe in a real God who brings real deliverance to real people in the real world.

Chapter 3

DEVELOPING SPIRITUAL
DISCERNMENT

S PIRITUAL DISCERNMENT IS one of the most difficult, and yet important, concepts to grasp and develop. It is an art, a developed skill, and, primarily, a gift from God. It is based in both the heart and the mind. Discernment is not merely founded in one's feelings, neither is it a purely cerebral exercise. It transcends human wisdom, yet at the same time requires mature thought. It cannot be summed up merely as common sense, and at the same time cannot defy what is clearly evident to any rational mind. Spiritual discernment must be founded in Scripture, but it must be Scripture that is informed and enlightened by the Holy Spirit. To say the least, it is a power to be trusted and relied upon, but always with the realization that it is not an exact science.

Spiritual discernment is the ability to assess people and situations, character and motives from a position of spiritual insight and intuition. However, spiritual discernment is not just knowing, or sensing something. It is knowing what to do with this insight and what, if any, action to take. It

THE WILL OF GOD

is the capacity to look beneath the surface and see what is not readily evident to the natural mind and senses. Jesus practiced spiritual discernment, and He also taught about its importance. In one of his prophecies about Jesus, Isaiah said, "He will not judge by what he sees with his eyes, or decide by what he hears with his ears" (Isa. 11:3). In John 7:24, Jesus Himself admonished people not to judge by appearances but to judge with righteous judgment.

Perhaps you have met someone who knew the Bible but seemed to have no real insight into the heart of God. Or maybe you have met someone who had a spiritual fervor and love for God, but was painfully uninformed about the Bible and the world. These types of deficiencies point us to some of the basic building blocks of discernment: knowledge and understanding, along with wisdom and insight.

Understanding the Bible and the wisdom of God is more than simply memorizing scriptures. We must be able to also understand the heart of God and have insight into His ways. For example, some musicians can only read the notes on the page but have no feel for the music or its movement. Other musicians disregard the sheet music and improvise so much that they are not even playing the same song anymore.

The Fear of the Lord

Spiritual discernment begins with the fear of the Lord. This truth is very important, and we can't walk in the will of God without it. Proverbs 9:10 teaches that "the fear of the LORD is the beginning of wisdom."

I learned something of what it means to live in the fear of the Lord in my relationship with my father. He was a

Christian, having been converted at a revival meeting in his teen years. He rarely talked about matters of faith, preferring instead to show his belief in God by his life. He was a very moral man, though his morality was not legalistic, nor was it a stifling presence that robbed the joy from our home. Simply put, he was a good man. His "religion" was to show up on time, keep his word, treat people with respect, and give an honest day's work for an honest day's pay. My father believed that a man should take care of his family and be faithful to his wife, and that is what he did in our home. He made an enormous impression on my life. It was clear that he loved his three boys. He was completely committed to us and to my mother. He loved to play and wrestle with us. He would lovingly squeeze my mother until she would say, "You're breaking my bones!"

My father wanted the best for my brothers and me. His expectations of us were reasonable, consistent, and easily understood. He would not tolerate dishonesty or outright rebellion. All the while, I never had one moment when I was afraid of him. I slept well at night. I never had to fear my father barging into my room in the middle of the night, dragging me out of bed, and beating me for no reason. I never had to contend with his demanding one thing one day and something completely different then next. I never doubted his love for me, and at the same time, I lived in continuous respect for his authority.

In a similar way, living in the fear of the Lord means that we do not have to spend one moment being afraid of God. His character is unchanging, and He is consistent, good, full of mercy, and incredibly kind. However, as we live under God's love and discipline, we also have a reverential fear of

Him because we know that He is God. Because He is God, He will not and cannot put up with willful disobedience or blatant rebellion. Living under the love and discipline of God is what the Bible calls the reverential fear of the Lord.

The fear of the Lord begins when we willingly submit ourselves to God's authority. To do that, we must first realize that He alone occupies the place of supremacy. At the same time we must be convinced that nothing matters more to God than the welfare of His children. In response to this, we must willingly bring ourselves under the sovereign authority and discipline of almighty God—it is not only the place of security, it is the position from which the blessing of God flows to and through us.

Emotional Maturity

Spiritual discernment cannot function apart from the Spirit of God. Genuine wisdom comes as a revelation from God and affects both the heart and the mind. There are, however, certain basic building blocks from which true discernment can begin to emerge. One of the most important foundations concerns maturity.

Emotional maturity is a prerequisite for spiritual discernment and the life that flows from it. To understand what this means, it is important that we recognize the selfish, superficial behavior of emotional immaturity. A person who has not grown beyond the immediate gratification of personal desires is emotionally stunted. Such a person has not yet developed into a giving person and sees the fulfillment of their own personal needs as their top priority in life. If we do not develop into whole persons who see that we have a purpose beyond our personal wants and needs, we remain emotionally immature. Immature persons see themselves as the center of their own universe whereas the goal of maturity is to be whole persons, able to give and receive in a healthy manner. As we learn to lovingly invest in the needs of others we grow in maturity. This is less a function of chronology and more a function of completeness or wholeness. It is important for us to become as whole as possible. This is why we have such a vital need of being in relationship with a healthy Christian community. We cannot learn to give and receive by ourselves. As we mature in our understanding of the vital necessity of functioning within community, we learn the value of proper authority, teamwork, and mutual interdependence.

Maturity has at its root the sense of growing up, but we certainly know many people who have aged but never matured. We also know some who are wise beyond their years. Ephesians 4:13 speaks about believers being built up, becoming mature, to the full measure and stature of Christ. In 1 Corinthians 13:11, Paul said that when he became a man, he gave up childish ways.

On one level, Scripture instructs us to become like children, to have a childlike faith and trust in God (Matt. 18:3). Child-like is not the same as child-ish. We are called to be mature so that we can prove ourselves worthy of God's trust. In Matthew 16:19, Jesus said to Peter, "I will give you the keys to the kingdom of heaven." What an incredible thing to do. If I were going to give someone the keys to my house, I would have to trust them implicitly. They would have the power to allow certain people in and keep others out. I would want them to take care of my home as if it was theirs.

Jesus was giving Peter the keys to life in the kingdom. He was entrusting him with task of proclaiming, by word and deed, the life of the kingdom of heaven—how to enter it, how to live in it, how it functions, and how to enable others to enter it. You do not give that kind of authority to irresponsible children!

This authority, which Jesus Christ has given to the church, has eternal implications. It also has important earthly ramifications, especially in its effect on the lives of people. This is why God will first give us just a little authority to see how we handle it. As Jesus explained in Luke 16:10–11, the one who is faithful in little things will be faithful in big things. Furthermore, if you are dishonest with a small amount of money, who will trust you with true riches?

People talk so much about trusting God, but here is an equally important question: can God trust us? In a healthy family, parents give their children responsibilities to the degree they demonstrate their ability to fulfill them. So it is with God and His gifts; the more we demonstrate maturity in the appropriate use of spiritual authority, the more we will receive it. Spiritual discernment is an important aspect of that kind of spiritual authority.

As we seek to grow in emotional maturity, many of us need inner healing so that we can move beyond self-centered living. So often, we act out of inner needs that compel us into living in ways we do not want. Healing can take place on many levels: physical, emotional, spiritual, and relational. Jesus wants to heal today as much as or more than He did when He walked the earth. If the healing of the body is miraculous, the healing of the heart is supernatural as well. My prayer for myself and others has always been, "Lord, please make us whole—on the inside especially—so that we may be free to give and receive love in a healthy manner. Help us, Lord, to mature to the place where we are no longer dominated by our own needs but serve others in Your Name."

The Whole Counsel of God

Growth in spiritual and emotional maturity brings wholeness and completeness to our lives. As we open ourselves to the whole counsel of God, we receive a growing level of spiritual discernment, are able to make mature decisions, and are positioned to live more complete lives. What you will find is that certain aspects of the life of faith resonate quite readily with you while others may not. For instance, you might love worship but not gravitate so quickly toward helping the poor; you might be keen on issues of doctrine but less apt to focus on love. While this is normal, it is important that we also make an effort to grasp those aspects of kingdom life that do not resonate so prominently in our thinking. As we seek God in this way, He will give wholeness to our understanding of the following questions:

Is the gospel personal or social?

Both are very important aspects of the gospel. On one hand, the gospel is a personal call for each of us to be converted through repentance and the knowledge of the Son of God. This conversion should manifest itself through changes in certain personal perspectives and behaviors: a life of faith in God and trust in God's promises, personal purity, prayer and worship, and love and service to others.

This aspect of the gospel affirms that God is love and God is holy.

The other side of the gospel has at its core the establishment of a just society that reflects the goodness and justice of God for all people. It proclaims that righteousness and justice are the foundations of the throne of God and denounces injustice, oppression, tyranny, and prejudice as anathema to the entire will and purpose of the Lord. This aspect of the gospel calls each of us to account by asking, How can you say that your heart is good if your actions are bad? How can you say you love God if you step over bleeding Lazarus lying at your very gate? (Luke 16:19–21). How can you claim spiritual integrity if you give deference to the rich at the expense of the poor? (James 2:1–4).

Unfortunately, the American church has divided itself into these two seemingly opposing sides: the so-called evangelical camp that focuses on personal conversion, and the so-called social camp that centers on social issues. It is a foolish and unnecessary fight because the two are not in opposition, but rather act as important parts of one complete whole. We cannot deal effectively with the spiritual lives of people if we ignore their obvious physical plight. Where the kingdom of God comes, there is healing and wholeness for individuals, and justice is sought and actively pursued.

How do we understand faith and works?

The Bible says that we are justified by faith alone (Rom. 5:1). "For by grace you have been saved through faith; and this is not your own doing, it is the gift of God" (Eph. 2:8, RSV). We enter the kingdom of heaven by faith in the fully atoning death and life-giving resurrection of Jesus Christ.

Yet the prophetic voice of the Bible cries out to us and asks, How can you say you are a faithful believer in God if your actions do not coincide with the life of faith? (James 2:17). How can you say you love God if you oppress your workers? (James 5:4). How can you say you love your brother if you do not do anything to help his situation? (James 2:15-16). How can you say you are fulfilling the life of faith if you pass by on the other side when your neighbor is in need? (Luke 10:29-37). Christianity is more than voting for the "right" candidates and placing a Bible on your desk or coffee table.

Through the whole counsel of God, we come to understand that the life of faith reigns both in our hearts and our actions. True righteousness is a gift of God, and at the same time it influences the way we live, the way we see the world, and the way we regard and treat other persons.

Should we emphasize law or grace?

The Bible proclaims both the law of God and also His love that was freely poured out in Christ. However, most of us have erred by focusing either on God's irrefutable commandments or on His incredible grace. We either slay people with God's laws or love them without the foundation of His commands. Ephesians 4:15 gives us the very wise counsel to "speak the truth in love." While this can often be one of the most challenging aspects of the life of faith, it is vitally important because love without truth is universalism, and truth without love is legalism. Love or truth without holiness is just plain hypocrisy. The love of God and the truth of God cannot be separated.

John 1:14 testifies that Jesus was "full of grace and truth." This was not some contrived balancing act or compromised combination of the two. He was, and is, 100 percent grace and 100 percent truth. He was and is the complete revelation of the love of God. He is a friend of sinners, forgiving, and forbearing. He is also righteous and holy, without blemish and fully obedient to the Father's will. Only Jesus can call people to account for their sin and still undergird them with redemptive love. He sees sin not just as a violation of the Father's laws but ultimately destructive to the ones He so dearly loves.

As we live more of our life in Christ, we can begin to grasp the full nature of the gospel and the completeness of the wisdom of God. That is why the Bible admonishes us to "grow up into him who is the head" (Eph. 4:15), to the full maturity of the nature and stature of Christ Himself (Eph. 4:13, RSV). If we are to strive to be complete, we must know that we are only "complete *in him*" (Col. 2:10, KJV, emphasis added).

Released by the Holy Spirit

We have laid the foundation for developing spiritual discernment through the fear of the Lord, emotional and spiritual maturity, and an understanding of the whole counsel of God. These are the building blocks of true wisdom. However, wisdom alone cannot give us spiritual discernment. It develops over time through the effectual working of the Holy Spirit in an individual who maintains such a foundation. All knowledge, intelligence, ability, and even the Bible itself lie dormant until the power of the Holy Spirit gives life and releases spiritual discernment.

In the final analysis, spiritual discernment is a gift God gives to those who can receive it and use it in an appropriate manner. When it is exercised, it is like all spiritual gifts, which work for the good of those who need it. It is not a random energy floating about the universe; it is the counsel of God, released through faithful stewards for the redemptive purposes of God. Having the Spirit of God functioning within you does not give you permission to do everything you please. Neither does it mean you will always be right and never wrong. Spiritual discernment is not an exact science. We must remain humbly dependent on God so we do not get too full of ourselves. Learning to discern things spiritually is exactly that: a learning process. There will be trials and errors. Personally, I have made many mistakes while thinking I was acting under the influence of God. But I have tried to learn from each one. Over time, you learn how and when the Spirit moves. You learn to listen. You learn that the Spirit of God is an extension of your relationship with Christ. Apart from Him you can do nothing (John 15:5).

Chapter 4

EXPERIENCING LIFE
IN THE SPIRIT

W HEN WE COME to Christ by faith, we are not simply adding Jesus to our existing life; we are entering into a new way of life under His direction. If Christ is to be our authority and empowerment, it naturally follows that He will exercise His authority by directing the way we live. He does this through the Holy Spirit.

Life in the Spirit is patently different than any other way of life. Yes, we maintain many of our normal activities; we still get up in the morning, go to work or school, relate to people, and make decisions. On the other hand, some of the things we do change because our priorities change. The way we set goals and make decisions is fundamentally different. Proverbs 3:5–6 says that if we commit our ways to the Lord, He will direct our paths. He does this by the indwelling presence of the Holy Spirit.

Changing from a self-directed life to life in the Spirit is not easy. Some of the basic tenets by which we live are almost opposite of those we have been following. At first it can even be frightening to let go of old ways and seek to establish God's way of life. But soon we find it remarkably liberating from the toil, striving, worry, and fear under which so many of us have lived. While we have an important part in how God's purposes unfold in us, the major responsibility is God's. If we allow it, the Lord Jesus will live His wonderful life through us.

The Holy Spirit is the full presence of God who indwells the body, mind, and spirit of the believer. He fulfills Christ's promise that He and the Father would come to make Their home within us (John 14:23). It may be helpful to visualize the Holy Spirit as the life of God flowing through us. God's blessing, nature, love, and power reside within us and flow through us like a river. Wherever the river of God's life flows, it brings life, healing, transformation, revelation, love, joy, unity, and peace (Ezek. 47:9).

I am not trying to paint some mythical picture or pie in the sky image of life in the Spirit. It will indeed manifest itself in the concrete realities of living. God will work in us and through us to accomplish divine purposes. Often, He will cut away that which does not honor God or that which is destructive to people.

The Holy Spirit is the source of our revelation, wisdom, and discernment. Through the Spirit, we are able to learn and appropriate truth, evaluate situations, and make decisions that are in keeping with the will of God. The Spirit is ever present with us to teach us all things and remind us of what Jesus has said (John 14:26). He takes what is Christ's and makes it known to us (John 16:15). Through the Spirit, God reveals His deepest thoughts and desires to us (1 Cor. 2:10).

The Spirit is more than a source of information; He is the source of God's power.

Acts 1:8 promises that we will receive power when the Holy Spirit has come upon us. According to Ephesians 1:19–20, this power is "like the working of [God's] mighty strength" that He used to raise Jesus from the dead and exalt Him to His place at God's right hand, far above every rule, power, and dominion. This power is not to be used in a gratuitous, self-serving fashion. Rather, it is given to us for our good and the good of others, to govern and guide us and to accomplish God's purposes on the earth.

God accomplishes His will on Earth through the Holy Spirit. For example, when God was preparing to send His Son into the world, He sent the angel Gabriel to Mary, the woman He had chosen to give birth to His Son. After Gabriel told her that she would give birth to Jesus, she asked how this could happen, since she was a virgin. Gabriel responded, "The Holy Spirit will come upon you and the power of the Most High will overshadow you" (Luke 1:35).

It was not Mary's task to go and get herself pregnant. Instead, she was called to cooperate with what God was doing and make herself an open vessel for His work. She also had to nurture the life of God's Son growing within her until He would be born through her. In much the same way, it is our job to allow God to conceive something within us, nurture it, and care for it until He births it through us.

This is one of the most important principles of Spirit-led living, and it is fundamentally different from our natural tendency which is this: try to figure out the will of God and then go do it. The will of God is actually something that unfolds as He gives birth to His plan for us by His power.

It requires our cooperation but in no sense do we do it on our own. As the Spirit of God begins to function in us, we will begin to see how He works through us. It is vital that we learn God's ways and cooperate with what we see Him doing by joining our efforts with His.

For God's life to properly flow through us as He intends, we must first of all be secure in who we are as God's children. Otherwise, we will forever live in doubt and fear and continuously try to prove ourselves or justify our own worthiness. Second Timothy 1:7 assures us that God has not given us a Spirit of fear, but "a spirit of power, of love and of self-discipline." When we are secure in our place among the children of God, we can more aptly change our focus from ourselves and our own needs to the needs of others. We can better help others discover their God-given identity and purpose.

This is a very important characteristic of life in the Spirit. If the Spirit is working in us, we should be making a noticeable change toward a more outward focus in our life. It is not that we totally abandon every personal desire and need, but that our personal desires be subservient to our commitment to bless other people. God loves people, and He brings tangibility to His love through those who walk in His ways and open themselves to His loving Spirit. Jesus came not to be served but to serve and to give His life for many (Matt. 20:28). The Spirit brings this same impetus into the lives of believers.

God works within our own creative abilities. We do not have to become someone patently different in our ideas, passions, and abilities. Why would God give us certain gifts and then demand that we abandon them to fulfill His divine purpose? He gave us those abilities for His purposes. It would be a shame to squander them on anything else. I like to think that when we give our lives to God, we become more of who we were created to be. Our abilities will be released in their full measure!

Romans 8:14–17 teaches that the Spirit assures us of our identity in Christ and gives us liberty from slavery to fear by the knowledge of God's deep and profound love for us. We are able, by the Spirit, to call God our heavenly Father and trust in His love. As we do this, His Spirit "testifies with our spirit that we are God's children." And if we are secure as God's children, we may rest assured that our destiny is in His loving hands. But where does this all begin? How do we begin to shift into this life in the Spirit?

Making the Shift

Access your spirit

God created us with three basic components: body, mind, and spirit. This may be an oversimplification, but it helps us begin to understand who we are and how we function. Most of us function within the realm of the body and the mind. We work to fulfill certain basic bodily needs such as food, rest, and shelter; we also contend with the frailties of the flesh, which may include lust, fatigue, and anger. We also function within our minds. Our thoughts determine to a large extent what we believe and what we do. The spiritual life of most people is confined to a mental process.

The third component within us—our spirit, our "heart"—affects us more than we realize. Have you ever thought something in your mind, but couldn't believe it in your heart? You may know in your head that God loves you but you have a difficult time convincing your heart. Perhaps you have been in a relationship that you knew in your head was wrong but you could not extricate your heart from it.

Life in the Spirit begins when we begin to access and exercise control over our spirit. Most of what God does in us will be through our spirit. God's work will inform our mind and have tangible effects on our actions, but the focal point will be the interaction of God's Spirit with ours. The issues of our lives proceed from our hearts. Our perspective, character, and behavior are largely determined from the content and disposition of our hearts.

We can, by a decision of our will, begin to access the spirit within us. This cannot be done in haste, and it requires a quietness of soul. Our hectic lifestyle often makes this difficult, but when we begin to spend time in quiet reflection, we can begin to access our hearts. Once we do this, it is important that we begin to open our hearts to the Lord. Prayer is not simply thinking about and asking God for things. It is opening our spirit to God and connecting our spirit with God's. The most vital work God does in us is Spirit-to-spirit. We pray with our minds; we also pray with our spirits. We sing to the Lord with our minds; we also sing with our spirits (1 Cor. 14:15).

Hear from God

I cannot overstate the importance of our connection and communion with God. Time spent in the presence of God and communing with Him in our mind and spirit—along with obedience—are the most vital components of the Spirit-led life. There is simply no substitute for time spent with God. It does not have to be a long period of time, but it must be time dedicated to God and spent in focused communion with Him. Again, it is time spent not just thinking about God but opening the deep place of your spirit.

Hearing from God is the birthright of each of God's children. It is inconceivable that our heavenly Father would require us to do His will without also providing the means by which that will is clearly communicated to us. Some maintain that God only speaks through the Bible or through the church, and these are certainly vital links. However, they are not the only ones. The Bible often refers to the revelation of God through the Spirit, and this is another vital means of communication available to us today, although we should never rely on it exclusively.

In much the same way we as infants learned the voice of our parents, we also need to learn the voice of God. We must learn to distinguish God's voice from our own thoughts or emotions. If you are not sure about what you might have heard from God, wait for confirmation. God speaks to us in the framework of what we can understand. As we attune our ears to God's voice, we will recognize when He is speaking to us.

We all process information differently and respond to different stimuli in different ways. Some of us are inclined toward the intellectual, and others are more relational. Some of us are verbal learners, some are visual, and others learn more by hands-on experience. Some see life in terms of straight lines and right angles while others see life with gentle shades and hues. Since God made us, He knows how our minds work and will speak to us in ways we can understand.

I want to caution you at this point. We cannot each do our own thing, claiming that this is the way God speaks to us. History is replete with abuses of those claiming to have heard from God. Instead, we must always remember that God's communication to all of us will have certain consistencies. He will not be one way with one person and another way with someone else. His will is always consistent with His Word. It is also important that we be in a healthy, mature, loving Christian fellowship where we can receive revelations of God that cannot be gained individually. This is an important check and balance, insuring that we do not go astray in our own personal spiritual insights.

We cannot have effectual communion with God if we are engaged in some other activity amidst the din of the world and our daily responsibilities. For this reason, it is vitally important that we set aside a time to meet with God in a quiet place where we can listen with our ears and eyes, and in the depths of our hearts. It is not enough just to read the Bible and say our prayers. We must learn to commune with God, opening our hearts to Him and inviting Him into every part of our lives. This is an important discipline of the Spirit-led life; over time it becomes something we excitedly anticipate doing.

It takes time for the Spirit of God to work in our hearts and minds, and we cannot hasten it. In our communion with God, we must quiet our minds. When our minds race unceasingly with one thought after another, it is hard for God to get a word in edgewise. However, we can hear Him speak as we learn to discipline our minds, slow our thoughts, and focus on His beauty and majesty.

At times, the Spirit will come to us in powerful, almost breathtaking ways which may prompt spontaneous praise from within our hearts. It is awesome when this happens. At other times, we will hear a still, small voice within us and recognize it as God's. Many times, we will hear God speak in our spirit and give life and special meaning to the words we are reading in the Bible.

If you are serious about desiring to move more into the Spirit-led life, then I suggest that you first read everything the Bible says about the Spirit and believe what you have read. There are a lot of misconceptions about the Spirit. Believe what the Bible says. Regularly ask God to fill you with His Spirit which is His life. You might even want to seek out a trustworthy believer to pray for you and with you about this. Then as you live your daily life, begin to obediently respond to what you believe God is leading you to do. Take small steps at first.

Seeking the Reality of God

Jesus promised that the Father would "give the Holy Spirit to those who ask Him" (Luke 11:13). Speaking of the Spirit in John 7:37, He said, "If anyone is thirsty, let him come to me and drink." The Spirit of God comes to us through our relationship with Jesus Christ. He does not work in us against our will, but He functions in us to the degree we allow. We can nurture His ministry in us by obeying Paul's instruction for Timothy to "fan into flame the gift of God, which is in you" (2 Tim. 1:6). We do this by actively seeking the Spirit's influence but also by exercising that influence through obedience to it. We have the power to quench the Spirit by refusing to allow Him to function (1 Thess. 5:19, NKJV), and we have the ability to grieve Him by our acts of disobedience and stubborn refusal (Eph. 4:30).

The Holy Spirit is directly involved in unfolding the will of God in our lives. Through the Spirit, God informs us of His will; and by the Spirit, He performs it. Our role is twofold: to *agree* with what God is doing and to *join Him* in the effort. Ephesians 2:10 explains that "we are God's workmanship, created in Christ Jesus to do good works." Philippians 2:13 adds that God is working "both to will and to do" the good pleasure of His purpose (NKJV). God plays the much larger role in performing His will, but our part is vital. If we fight it or refuse to comply, how difficult it is for the will of God to be accomplished in us!

Second Timothy 3:5 warns against a disturbing hindrance to the ministry of the Holy Spirit when it describes some people as "having a form of godliness but denying its power." In other words, they go through the motions of Christian faith but deny God's supernatural power to transform lives and situations. They do this by saying that the power of the Holy Spirit was for another time and is no longer relevant to us today as it was in Biblical times. They also teach that the gifts are no longer manifested as they were in the early church and that the miracles of God no longer happen.

If these things were true—which they are not!—we open the door to the possibility that other parts Bible were for another time and no longer relevant to us. While there may indeed be aspects of the Bible which must be understood in terms of their culture and time, we must be very careful. We can't pick and choose what we are going to believe according to our own preconceived notions. When we let go of biblical truth, we cast ourselves adrift in a sea of hopelessness. The miracles of God are not confined to history. If you can believe in the miracle of God's love for you and God's saving grace in Christ, you can believe *every* miracle He promises to perform. In John 14:12, Jesus said, "I tell you the truth, anyone who has faith in me will do what I have been doing. He will do even greater things than these, because I am going to the Father." Before He went to the Father, Jesus was confined to the limitations of a physical body. He could only be in one place at a time. He could teach people about the life of faith; He could do little to assist them in it. By going to the Father, He opens the door to coming to us through the Holy Spirit. Not only can He then be in all places at once, He can live within those who seek Him. The life of faith is no longer an external requirement imposed on us but the life of Jesus Himself lived in and through us!

In response to God's promises to give us His Spirit, we must open our lives to the Father and invite the Spirit to come in. Oh, how it pleases the Father to give us His Spirit in ever-increasing measure. Let us ask not just once but again and again as an expression of our desire for an infilling of God's life. It is important that we seek the reality of God more than a thrilling experience. Let us look for every available opportunity to receive God's blessings and respond immediately and enthusiastically when He reveals His presence and power.

God can do great things through us as we open ourselves fully to the Spirit of God. The Bible frequently likens the Holy Spirit to wind—the breath of God—and water—living water, the river of life. Like wind and water, the Spirit always moves toward the place of least resistance. If we resist the Spirit, He will not be free to work. If our rational minds refute what is clearly taught in Scripture, we will always stumble and rarely walk in the power of the full counsel of God. If we have areas of reserve, mentally or physically, it may be difficult to see things from God's perspective.

John the Baptist referred to the work of Jesus by saying, "He will baptize you with the Holy Spirit" (Matt. 3:11). *Baptize* means literally to cover wholly with a fluid or "immerse." When we are baptized in the Holy Spirit, the Spirit pervades and influences every area of our lives: heart, body, thoughts, dreams, ambitions, and decisions. We will be hindered in our walk with God if we reserve any part of who we are from God's influence. We may achieve a certain level of spiritual insight and authority, but it will be limited. The Spirit will function to the degree we abandon ourselves to God. You can determine the extent to which God works in and through you. Churches can determine the extent to which God will effectively work through them as well.

The work of the Holy Spirit to create true, lasting change in us is a process. When the Spirit of God came at Pentecost, it was a beginning point, just as our relationship with Jesus had a point of introduction. Life in the Spirit has a beginning point as well. You cannot simply wait around hoping something will happen. You must pursue God and God's spiritual blessings. Just as we spend the rest of our lives developing our relationship with Christ, we experience an ever-increasing flow of the Spirit and His power. If we are serious about our spiritual life, we will journey through places of challenge and places of major breakthrough. God will lead us from victory to victory, from one degree of glory to another as we are "transformed into his likeness" (2 Cor. 3:18).

This cannot happen by accident any more than sleeping with a book under our pillows will increase our knowledge. I remember a time when I considered myself open to the gifts of the Spirit and was quite proud of the fact that I was not like the so-called closed-minded traditionalists who resisted the Spirit of God. And then I read 1 Corinthians 14:1, "Make love your aim, and earnestly desire the spiritual gifts, especially that you may prophesy" (rsv). I was convicted. Growth in the Spirit of God would not happen to me if I just passively waited for it and did nothing. I had to be proactive. I had to desire, hunger, thirst, learn, seek, ask, knock, and pursue the things of the Spirit.

The Power of Healing Prayer

Healing takes many forms: physical, emotional, spiritual, and relational. I have often said that it is a marvelous thing when Jesus heals a person's body, but it is more amazing and wonderful when God heals a human heart. And it is even more glorious when a relationship is healed!

Francis and Judith MacNutt of Christian Healing Ministry (CHM) are precious people who have tapped into the power of healing prayer, and their ministry has greatly impacted my life. Healing prayer is not some strange version of praying. It is simply a process of praying with others by which we allow God to shed light on our lives and perhaps to bring healing to some emotional wounds. My wife had gone to CHM for several days of healing prayer, and it had done wonders for her. Like all good wives, she suggested that

I should go too. She said that I needed it. I didn't think I needed it, and I wanted her to leave me alone. I had serious reservations about what I thought were the touchy-feely aspects of the faith. At some point, however, I had to come to terms with the fact that I was not living with the patience and love I knew I needed and wanted. Wounds from the past and my own response to those wounds were causing me to live out certain unhealthy behaviors. So I finally signed up and went.

As I drove to Jacksonville, Florida, to participate in an intensive time of inner healing prayer, the Lord spoke to my heart, *"We aren't going to have any problems down there are we?"*

I knew what God meant. God does not have to say many words for me to get the picture. He was telling me that I was not to go down there and waste people's time by being a jerk, closing myself off, and refusing to fully participate in the process. It would have been easy for me to go through the motions but not fully allow the process to penetrate to my deepest needs. Pride and fear can often govern us and severely limit God's blessing.

That day I was at least smart enough to answer the Lord, "No, Sir, we won't have any problems." I resigned to give myself fully to the process and allow God to do everything He wanted to accomplish in me.

When I arrived at CHM, I was teamed up with two precious prayer ministers. They did not function as counselors but lovingly helped me pray and open my life to the healing power of God. They were gentle and kind and did not push me. The prayer sessions were private and confidential. What I remember most was that the atmosphere surrounding our sessions was totally devoid of judgment. It was a safe setting that fostered trust and the ministry of the pure love of God. I felt like I could have confessed any sin to them, and they would have simply said, "Let's take it to the Lord and see what He wants to do with it." The only thing that seemed to matter to the prayer ministers was that I be whole.

I had to allow God into my heart to heal my broken places. I had to give Him access to my feelings of shame and fully trust that He would not embarrass or hurt me. God did a deep work of healing in my spirit those three days. It was not the end-all answer to every pain or problem in my life, but I knew I had allowed God to begin a process of healing that would continue not only in my heart and mind, but also in my physical being.

On the last day, Judith MacNutt prayed for each of us who had been participating in the prayer ministry. I watched as, one-by-one, people went forward, and she gently placed her hand on them and prayed for them. Although I could not overhear what she was praying, I saw the results. As she prayed, each person went down in what is sometimes called "resting in the Spirit." I had seen this in charismatic meetings and even in some worship services in which I had taken part. However, I had never personally experienced it until that day. Normally, I would have bolted from the room, but I remembered my promise to God and stayed.

Eight people went up to the altar, and all eight went down. I was number nine. Judith, who is quite a bit shorter than my six-foot eight-inch frame, smiled up at me as I stood before her. I sensed that people behind me were scrambling for safety. When she reached up and gently touched my face, she said, "Kent, I anoint you with the precious love of Jesus Christ."

I felt the Spirit come over me and gently begin to lay me down. Instinctively, I braced myself to try to remain upright, but God said to my heart, "Don't resist. Let Me have you."

In obedience to God, I let go, and the loving hands of some people behind me gently laid me down on the floor. I was not down very long when I felt a kind of giddiness within myself. I actually began to chuckle as I thought, "Look at the big proud man now!" In my spirit, I asked the Lord, "Can I get up now?"

God replied, "Yes, I'm finished."

"What happened, Lord?" I asked

"I have implanted within you something that I want you to nurture," God answered. "It will grow within you. It is very good."

In that moment in Jacksonville, Florida, I had what for a man must be the closest feeling to being pregnant. God imparted the life of the Son of God deep within me, just as He did in Mary, the mother of Jesus. But I first had to let God have control over my body. For God to effectively work out His will in us, He has to be able to function fully within our total being. We do not worship and serve the Lord only with our minds and hearts, but also with our bodies.

My life did not become perfect that day. Interestingly enough, not long after that experience I began to face some of the most difficult challenges of my life. But something within me had changed. I had opened the depths of my spirit to God, and His Spirit had gladly come in. It was not a one-time affair. Since then, I have opened myself again and again.

My desire is for Jesus to be Lord over my own heart, mind, and body so that He can function more freely and completely in me.

The results have been gradual, but I have experienced a positive change in my attitude toward myself and others. Perhaps those around me can be more objective witnesses if there has been a true change in my behavior. However, I know that God has softened my heart in many ways. Now I am able to be more loving, especially toward my wife and children. God has become more real and powerful to me. It has taken a while for all my ungodly behavior to disappear, and it is by no means completely gone. But after my experience in Florida, I began to make serious progress toward the life of godliness and love I so desired.

God imparts life in us, and our part is to nurture it until it is born as the work of the Spirit of God. The ministry of the Spirit within us and through us does not give us carte blanche to do anything we please. Neither does it mean that we will always be right. As we live in the Spirit and learn to be spiritually discerning, we must remain humbly dependent on God so we do not get too full of ourselves. Over time, we learn how and when the Spirit moves. We learn to listen to Him and give ourselves fully to Him in our relationship with Christ. Apart from Christ, we can do nothing (John 15:5).

The Spirit-flowing Life

The Spirit-filled life has traditionally been characterized by the image of a bucket that has to be continually filled, usually in church, so one can go out into the world pouring out God's love to those around them. This analogy is not consistent with Scripture, and it is not a very efficient way of doing business. If I had to water a garden by carrying untold numbers of buckets out to it, I would immediately get myself a hose.

The Spirit-filled life would be more appropriately called the "Spirit-flowing" life. When the Bible talks about the Spirit, it is referring to the life of God living in us and flowing through us. There are certain characteristics of this life. It is an abundant life which means a plentiful supply, a quality life and an exceedingly good life. Jesus said, "I have come that they may have life, and that they may have it more abundantly" (John 10:10, NKJV). The life of God is eternal. When we are born again in Jesus' name, we are born into eternal life (John 5:24). The gift of eternal life is not something we receive when we die; it is not the door prize as we exit this world.

As God's life lives in us, it brings healing, wholeness, power, and love. As it flows through us, it takes this blessing to others. Ezekiel 47 talks about the river of God also called the river of life. Wherever the river flows, things begin to live (Ezek. 47:9). Even in the most difficult, hopeless, situations, the river of God's life brings life! It is that same life which can flow through us. Jesus said, "He who believes in me, as the scripture has said, 'Out of his heart shall flow rivers of living water'" (John 7:38, RSV).

It makes a lot of sense to see each of us as a hose through which the life of God flows. A hose has three jobs: stay connected, stay open, and stay pliable. A hose cannot manufacture one drop of water, and neither can you or I manufacture the life of God. Our task is to simply stay connected to the Source. A hose that is not connected to the source of water is not much good for anything. If we do not abide in Jesus, we are pretty much useless and, like dead branches, will whither and die. My primary task as a child of God is to stay continuously connected to the Source of life. My very life depends on times of personal and corporate worship and prayer. We don't just believe in Jesus, we draw our very sustenance from Him.

A hose has to stay open or it is not much good to anybody. When sin clogs our hose, it impedes the flow of God's life. So does a closed mind or a closed heart. Refusing to believe God and His Word is a stubborn resistance that hinders the ministry of the Spirit.

A hose has to stay pliable. A stiff, rigid hose may be somewhat useful, but it is a major pain to move it. Refusing to do what God wants us to do constitutes a rigidity that greatly limits our spiritual effectiveness. God's Spirit will not force us to do anything. We must choose to obey Him. Jesus said, "Why do you call me 'Lord, Lord,' and not do what I say?" (Luke 6:46). The Spirit often speaks to us in a still, small voice, and it is important that we listen. If we don't, we may live to regret it.

Deep Calls to Deep

The will of God is not a mystery. God has gone to great lengths to reveal His will to humanity, and He has not withheld any of Himself in the process. Colossians 1:19 says that "God was pleased to have all his fullness dwell in [Christ]." John 1:18 declares, "No one has ever seen God, but God the One and Only, who is at the Father's side, has made him known." And in John 14:9 Jesus told His disciples, "He who has seen me has seen the Father" (RSV).

First Corinthians 2:10 teaches that the Spirit searches God's heart—His deepest thoughts, desires, and plans. We, too, have access to the depths of God's heart by the same Spirit. This does not mean that we have God figured out. However, we are assured that God does not remain shrouded in mystery. If God wants us to do His will—and He does— it would be inconceivable to believe He would expect us to guess at it. We do not need to stumble about in the darkness hoping to get it right.

The Spirit also knows the depths of our hearts. He knows us at an intensely deep level, even better than we know ourselves. Consequently, He is able to pray for us in ways that we are unable to articulate. He brings the depth of the heart of God together with the depth of who we are (Rom. 8:26–27). Most of the work God does in us is Spirit to spirit. As Psalm 42:7 says, "Deep calls to deep."

Much of what God performs in us will be at a deeper level than we can cognitively grasp. We may not always be aware of the ways God is working in us, and others may even notice positive changes in our attitudes and behavior before we do. It is so important that we allow God to do a deep and lasting work in us. Superficial prayers yield superficial results, and shallow worship touches only the surface. It is important to cultivate the ability to lift our spirit to the Lord in times of personal and corporate worship and prayer.

The Holy Spirit is always present with us, but at certain times He makes His presence known in ways that go deeper than the level of our conscious mind. We must learn to seek and recognize these times when there is a unique sense of

God's presence, and we must respond by opening our spirit and our mind to God. There is a time to read the Bible, and there is a time to not read, but rather to seek God in our hearts. There is a time to speak and a time to listen. There is a time to simply wait upon God and, when He comes, to commune with Him.

Many times, the Spirit of God comes in waves. There is often an ebb and flow like the waves of the seashore. Sometimes we make the mistake of praying until we feel the presence of God and then quitting. However, the coming of the presence of the Lord is not the end, but the beginning. It is the starting point. In these moments, it is vital that we continue to press on in prayer and into the heart of God. We must open our hearts to hear from God and seek a deeper level of union with Him. This is where the real work of the Spirit is done. He will take us to even greater levels of revelation and a deeper work in our character. This is the place of real change.

Chapter 5

BEING LED BY THE LORD

B
EING LED BY the Lord begins by obeying His commands, but it is so much more than that. It is being under His leadership day-by-day and even moment-by-moment in the everyday affairs of life. Christianity is not a religion—it is a way of life. Living life day-by-day under the guidance of the Lord is a foundational principle of our life in Christ.

It is one thing to have faith, but it is another thing altogether to live by faith (Rom. 1:17). We can have a wonderful faith in God that resides in our hearts but never sees the light of day because we never act on it. I am not just talking about involving ourselves in ministry in our churches or loving one another. I am talking about making personal life decisions on the basis of our beliefs about God. And what's more, I am talking about making life decisions based on what we believe we have heard from God.

We must acknowledge the fact that many grievous errors and even malicious acts have been committed by those who speak of "hearing from God" and "being led by the Lord." Yet, this does not refute the reality that God can and does speak to us and lead us. The wrong actions of some should not deter us from listening for God's voice. Their irresponsibility serves as a warning to be careful about the danger of acting in haste and failing to adequately think things through as we seek to follow God's leading.

Making Decisions

We make decisions all the time. Some of them are life-altering choices about marriage, employment, or our place of residence. Others are smaller, everyday decisions about our specific priorities or our response to a person or a situation. It would be nice if God would speak to us audibly or send us daily emails to give us our marching orders. Instead, the decisions we make, regardless of their apparent impact, are expressions of our relationship with God and the way He is shaping our character and revealing His will to us.

Many times we make the mistake of waiting until a crisis comes before we seek God with frantic, desperate prayers. Since God abounds in steadfast love and mercy, He will answer every cry of our heart. However, if we are in great emotional disarray, it will be difficult for us to hear God's voice. It is much better if we do not wait until we have a crisis to develop a relationship with God in which the leading of the Spirit is close at hand. We will be much more keenly aware of God's presence and leading if we have spent time with Him in close, daily communion and prayer.

The decisions we make are the direct result of the content of our character. Our decisions reflect the priorities, goals, and ambitions by which we live. When we are carnal in our nature and our thoughts, our goals reflect that carnality. As

God forms His life in us, our inner nature and thoughts are more oriented to kingdom living and godly purity. Our decisions will then begin to reflect His glory.

Some decisions are very difficult, and we make them with great prayer and supplication. However, as Isaiah 26:7 says, "The path of the righteous is level." As we grow into a deeper relationship with the Father and stability in our affection toward Him, we will have less anxiety about the direction and outcome of our lives. Even in the turbulence of a difficult decision, we can rest in God's unfailing faithfulness and the assurance that He will direct our paths.

The favor of the Lord rests unceasingly on the righteous, and God is always acting on behalf of those whose hearts trust in Him. This does not mean that we are immune from the perils that afflict all humanity, nor does it mean that He loves only those who love Him back. However, it does mean that God is well aware of everything we face. He cares deeply for us, and He will be faithful to open doors of opportunity for us in our times of desperate need.

One of the biggest mistakes we make is failing to wait on the Lord. We often try to kick open a door prematurely instead of waiting patiently for the Lord to open it on our behalf. I have found that most often, God is more concerned about what is going on *in* us than what is happening in the circumstances *around* us. While He cares about our struggles, the development of our virtue, and our faith, our relationship with God is more important to Him. As God works out His plans for us, He is working more diligently to produce genuine faith and godliness in us. These qualities last forever, while our external circumstances are temporary.

We make some decisions on the run every day, and we need to pray for God's daily guidance in this. At times, I have disregarded the promptings of the Spirit in these decisions, and it has proved costly. When we wait on the Lord for direction in major decisions, we need to hold them up to Him each day. Sometimes we have to hold them up to Him for many days. As we wait for Him to show us the way in His timing, He will be faithful to guide us. We will know the path to take, even if it is a difficult one. The main thing to always remember is that our relationship with God is more important than anything else. If we listen, we can hear God say, "My child, I am aware of your situation. This is about you and Me. Get your focus on to Me. Trust Me!"

Keeping the Commandments

Honoring and keeping the commandments of God is a necessary foundation for the Spirit-led life. It is the starting point that applies to everyone. No one is above the law, and we will never become so anointed of God that His rules do not apply to us any more. It is true that the apostle Paul said we are no longer "under the law, but under grace" (Rom. 6:14, KJV). However, he was not implying that the just and righteous commands of God no longer applied to those who live by the Spirit. Instead, he meant that Christ has set us free from the burden of religious perfectionism (Rom. 8:2). He has abolished vain traditions set by religious people who taught them as if they were legitimate commands of God.

Jesus fully atoned for our sin, and we no longer have to constantly atone for ourselves. We are free from the frantic obsession of trying to do things in a vain attempt to feel worthy and accepted. We are "accepted in the Beloved" (Eph. 1:6, NKJV) and have been made worthy through His cleansing. We are God's beloved children (1 John 3:2) through faith Christ, and we can rest in the knowledge that we are reconciled to Him.

All this does not mean, however, that God's rules no longer apply to us. Some of the best servants of God have fallen when they got arrogant and felt like the rules did not apply to them any more. The difference is that now the laws of God are no longer external requirements imposed on us, but they have now become the internal basis for the formation of our character. What the Spirit tells us will never supersede God's commands.

Agreeing With the Word

The Bible teaches that there is power in agreement. Jesus said that if even two of us agree about anything, it shall be done for us by our Father in heaven (Matt. 18:19). The power of God flows most perfectly when people are of one heart, one mind, and one accord. That is why there is no such thing as a vote in the kingdom of God. We come to consensus. We come to agreement. Division among people will thwart the flow of God's life as readily as sin does. The word "Amen" is not another word for "The End" to bring finality to a prayer. The word "Amen" actually means "so may it be." Your Amen is your consent. It is your agreement with the sentiment and statement of the prayer, action, or whatever is being expressed. When there is such agreement, the power of God is set free in that setting. Thus, it should not surprise us that there will always be complete agreement between the leading of the Spirit and the Word of God. The Spirit, the Word, and Jesus are always in agreement.

As we read the Scriptures, we also see the power of agreement revealed in the relationship between the Father and the Son. Jesus never disagrees with the Father. He not only obeys His heavenly Father, but He is in complete agreement with Him. He believes fully in what the Father is doing and sees the wisdom in it. In John 10:30 Jesus declared, "I and My Father are one" (NKJV). This statement teaches two important truths. First, Jesus is of the same nature and substance as the Father. God desires also that this be true of us: that we are recreated into the same form and likeness of God. Second, it shows that Jesus is in complete agreement with the Father. He only does "what He sees His Father doing" (John 5:19), and He only says what His Father tells Him to say (John 8:28). He is completely and totally in agreement with God, and it is His utter joy to do so.

My wife and I are blessed to have three children. All of them are terrific, well adjusted, productive, personable people and we are very proud of them. Like all parents, we had our moments of stress as our kids were growing up, especially during their teen years. We had pretty specific rules in our house. We tried not to be unreasonable and repressive, but we had to be responsible parents, especially since we were attempting to raise our children in a godly way. We told them that we must always know where they were and who they were with. They had a curfew, even when many of their friends did not. They also had to report in, even when many of their friends did not. Fortunately our children were for the most part obedient to the rules of the house. But they did not always agree with them. They may agree with those rules now that they are grown, but not then. Being one with God means that you not only obey God's commands, but you are also in complete agreement with them. Some people obey reluctantly or with anger and resentment. That is better than not obeying at all, but it is far better not only to obey but to be in agreement.

The Spirit of God will never lead us to do something that conflicts with the Word of God because they are both in perpetual agreement. For example, I have actually encountered misguided individuals who claimed that the Lord was telling them to leave their spouses and enter into an adulterous relationship. How could anyone possibly justify that kind of behavior? The great heartache that follows such deception and sin can be avoided if we will simply step back and examine our actions and motives against what God has said in the Word—the whole council of God. We must not discard the foundation of the commandments of God.

Deception happens in subtle, insidious ways. When I was in college, I was pretty wild. I was on my own for the first time, and I did not handle it well. Except for the grace of God, my life could have taken a permanent downturn and very well might have ended altogether. I can vividly remember one night when I told myself, "I am having so much fun; how can this be wrong?" Isn't it amazing how we can be deceived by our own logic! Unfortunately, when we are in the midst of our error, we often do not see it.

As I mentioned earlier, the Spirit searches the deepest things of the heart of God, and He knows the depths of the will of God. The Bible also tells us that the Spirit intercedes for us "in accordance with God's will" (Rom. 8:27). He is able to articulate the deepest needs of our hearts as He prays for us in perfect harmony with the will of the Father. Wouldn't you like to know what the Spirit is praying for you? Since the Spirit of God is in complete agreement with the Word of God, we can consult the Bible to gain insights into what He is praying for us. As we reflect on the Word in our times of personal prayer and devotion, it will come alive to us in its application to specific issues in our lives.

Let me share with you one example from Paul's prayer in Ephesians 3:16–19:

> I pray that out of his glorious riches he may strengthen you with power through his Spirit in your inner being, so that Christ may dwell in your hearts through faith. And I pray that you, being rooted and established in love, may have power, together with all the saints, to grasp how wide and long and high and deep is the love of Christ, and to know this love that surpasses knowledge—that you may be filled to the measure of all the fullness of God.

Is it not reasonable to claim this prayer as God's will for us as well as the Ephesian church? We can have confidence that God wants the same for us—that the Spirit, through the Word of God, is praying that for us as well. Imagine that! We can say "amen" to this prayer and come into agreement with the will of the Father, the Spirit, and the Word.

Knowing the will of God is one thing; agreeing with it is another. If you really did know God's will for you, are you sure you would agree with it? I can promise you that the will of God for your life is far better than your will for yourself. When we commit our ways to the Lord, we can have the full assurance that God is for us and not against us.

We commit our ways to God because we trust His unfailing wisdom and goodness.

I have no idea what the will of the Lord is for you. The Bible promises suffering and blessing, huge cost and tremendous benefit, as we follow the path of life. Abraham became very wealthy. Jesus had little or nothing materially. David was king. Paul went from trial to trial and beating to beating. Esther was queen. Mary became the mother of salvation. Joseph ruled pharaoh's kingdom. Jeremiah was an exile. Don't play games with God. Do not ask Him to tell you His will and then decide if you are in or out. Walking by faith means we have committed our way to the Lord and we will serve and praise Him without wavering or turning back.

Waiting on God

Living in the will of God involves not only a sense of what to do but also the understanding of when to do it. If we try to do the right thing at the wrong time, it is the same as doing the wrong thing. We are always ready for the next step long before God is. However, if we become impatient and do not wait on the Lord, we will suffer grief and regret. Even if our efforts succeed, they will not fulfill the eternal good that God intended.

Waiting on God is not a passive activity. The biblical characters Abraham and David learned this as they waited on God, and their lives also gave witness to the amazing way God works when we wait. In Genesis 15:5, God gave Abraham a promise that he would be the father of a multitude of people. It was many years until the miraculous birth of Isaac, but God was not inactive during those years (Gen. 18:9–15; 21:1–8).

First Samuel 30 tells how David, king of Israel, faced one of the most difficult times of his life. The Amalekites had attacked his home while he and his men were away. They had made off with all their property and their families. David's men were so angry that they were almost ready to stone him. It seemed that everything he had worked for was falling apart in front of his very eyes. Virtually helpless to do anything about it, "David strengthened himself in the LORD His God" (1 Sam. 30:6).

What does it mean to wait on the Lord? How does God strengthen us in those times? Here are some important considerations which I believe are part of how we strengthen ourselves in the Lord:

Acknowledge Who God Is

We must first learn to acknowledge the nature and goodness of God through the vehicle of praise. It should be part of our daily lives, and it should preface all our actions. It reminds us of the sovereignty of almighty God, especially in times of crisis, and it releases His power in every situation.

Worship and prayer enable us to be strengthened in the Lord. When we are battling for our lives, worship is crucial to our success! In Psalm 18:2, David testified: "The LORD is my rock, my fortress and my deliverer; my God is my rock, in whom I take refuge; He is my shield and the horn of my salvation, my stronghold."

Draw Close to God

One of the biggest mistakes we make is to act in haste and take matters into our own hands when things seem out of control. However, these are times when God wants to teach us to wait on Him. Psalm 27:14 says, "Wait for the LORD, be strong and take heart and wait for the LORD." In Psalm 33:20 the psalmist declared, "We wait in hope for the LORD." And Psalm 130:5–6 echoes, "I wait for the Lord, my soul waits, and in his word I put my hope. My soul waits for the Lord more than the watchman waits for the morning."

Waiting on God does not mean that we sit idly while things spin out of control. As we wait, our eyes and ears should be attuned to the heart of God. Sometimes the Lord will tell us to move forward, and other times He will tell us to wait until we see Him move first. If He makes us wait, He has a reason. Perhaps He wants to do something *in* us before does something *through* us. Instead of squandering our time of waiting, we need to draw close to God day by day and seek to learn what He wants to teach us. Difficult times are often critical times of spiritual growth.

Exodus 40:36–37 tells how the children of Israel learned to wait on God as He guided them by the cloud symbolic of His presence in their journey through the wilderness. When the cloud settled over a place, they made camp and remained there as long as it remained—for a day or a week or a month or a year. When the cloud lifted, they broke camp and followed it. They could do nothing to move the cloud, and their failure to follow it would only cause them to lose their way.

Waiting on God means that we ask Him what we should do. In 1 Samuel 30:7-8 David inquired of the Lord, and we too must rely on God's guidance when we make decisions. If He wants us to act immediately, He will show us. At such times, we can move forward with certainty that He will give us success. However, if He cautions us to wait, we must learn to wait until we receive clear direction from God. The absence of a green light is a red light. But once the way is clear, we need not be afraid to move forward!

Receive Comfort From the Holy Spirit

The Holy Spirit gives us supernatural, inexplicable comfort and strength from the presence of the Almighty. He comes to us as the true and living God to touch our hearts with the unfathomable love of "the Father of compassion and the God of all comfort, who comforts us in all our troubles" (2 Cor. 1:3-4). The apostle Paul prayed for this precious comfort of the Holy Spirit when he said, "I pray that he may strengthen you with power through his Spirit in your inner being" (Eph. 3:16).

When God instructed Joshua to prepare to lead the people of Israel into the land He had promised them, He said, "I will never leave you nor forsake you" (Josh. 1:5). The psalmist David received a similar assurance from God and confidently stated, "Though my mother and father forsake me, the LORD will receive me" (Ps. 27:10). And Jesus confirmed that God's presence will provide comfort to us by the Holy Spirit, whom the Father would give (John 14:16-18). He said, "I will not leave you as orphans; I will come to you" (v. 18).

God will come to us as surely as the dawn follows the darkness. Because of His promise to be with us, we do not need to be afraid. He will comfort us with His presence, and He will comfort us through other people. It is part of His ministry to us as we wait on Him.

Walk in the Unwavering Assurance That God Is Good

As we learn to wait on the Lord, we also learn to walk with an immovable faith in the love of God and complete trust in His faithfulness. This is what happened in the life of Abraham, who "did not waver through unbelief regarding the promise of God, but was strengthened in his faith and gave glory to God, being fully persuaded that God had power [and was willing] *to do what he had promised*" (Rom. 4:20–21, emphasis added). This same faith can also be the testimony of our lives.

These are not simply irrelevant Biblical concepts; they are integral to the life of faith. If you walk with God, you will be challenged. Do not be fooled into believing that if you live the life of faith that everything will always work out the way you want. In fact, sometimes the opposite happens. Hardship and difficulty will come. These are the most important times to implement the strategies of the Lord. First remember who God is as the great and mighty Lord of heaven and earth. Draw close to God by faith. Be determined that a time of crisis will not lead you away from God but will draw you closer to Him. Ask God to comfort you with His presence and even in those times when you do not feel that presence, rest in the unwavering assurance that God is good and that He will never forsake you.

Seeking Wisdom

As we seek to follow the leading of the Lord, it is important to cultivate our ability to hear His voice through all available avenues. For instance, God often uses my wife to speak to me. Many times when I have told her that I was about to do something she has inevitably asked, "Have you prayed about it?" This used to drive me crazy until I realized how right she was. Now I try to remember to ask God about everything. We are God's children, and if the details of our lives are important to us, they are important to God.

Sometimes we try to discern the will of God through the eyes of Scripture but are still unsure of what do. When this happens, we must look carefully at the choices before us and try to envision where they might lead and what they might produce. As we count the cost of a decision, we might make a list of the pros and cons, develop a flow chart, and make the most rational decision possible. This approach may have some value, but it is limited.

The will of God is not always rational according to our way of thinking. The Bible speaks of many faithful people who based their decisions on the leading of God, even when it did not seem purely rational. Abraham left Ur not knowing where he was going. Noah built the ark during a drought. Samuel chose David even when there were other seemingly more powerful men available. Esther went in to see the king at the risk of death. All of these decisions defy conventional wisdom. But these were not rash, foolhardy, misguided individuals. They were courageous men and women of faith. We will always face risks when we follow the will of God. Those who are afraid of taking risks will never get out of the boat and walk on water (Matt. 14:28–31).

Following God is not for the fainthearted, but neither is it for the foolish. I have seen tragic results of misguided people who gave themselves to foolhardy expressions of spirituality. This is why we must ask God to give us wisdom. James 1:5 promises that He will give it to us freely. James 3:17 helps us with a framework for godly wisdom so that we might think through the decisions we make to see where a certain decision might take us: "The wisdom from above is first pure, then peaceable, gentle, open to reason, full of mercy and good fruits, without uncertainty or insincerity."

This verse can help form the foundation of sound decision-making. According to this verse, if our decisions and deeds truly reflect the wisdom from God, they will be:

Pure: (from the same word as "holy" or "consecrated) clean, innocent, chaste, and undefiled

God will not lead us into immorality. The things of God are not shady, hidden, or subversive; neither should we be in the things we do. Decisions based on this kind of purity are not mixed with some evil intent. You might ask yourself this question, "Is this decision of mine innocent and without a hint of malice or evil intent?"

Peaceable: quiet, at rest, not intentionally causing disorder, not purposefully contentious

This verse is not a guarantee that we will have instant peace in our hearts about every decision we make. God may lead us into something that will bring us great turmoil because it challenges us or refutes our preconceived ideas. His may cut against the grain of our desires or challenge certain social norms. Nonetheless, a decision based on this principle will not have at its core the intent to cause harm, contention, or disorder.

We cannot expect every decision we make to give us a sense of inner peace. Not all decisions based on the will of God carry this type of confirmation.

For example, I have a good friend who is an attorney and a Spirit-led Christian. During his final year of law school, a prestigious law firm in a major city offered him a position that would be the fulfillment of any law student's dream. Yet, because he felt that God was leading him in a different direction, my friend declined the opportunity.

Years later, when he told this story to a group of law students, one of them commented, "I suppose you had peace about your decision."

"Peace?" my friend replied, "I had no sooner left the firm and I began to ask myself, 'Are you crazy? Do you have any idea what you just did?' No—I did not have any peace at all. But I believed I was doing was the right thing."

Jesus modeled the fact that the will of God is peaceable—that is to say, neither intentionally contentious nor purposefully determined to rebel against someone else. Although He was not afraid of confrontation, it was not His primary motivation. When Jesus responded to needs and situations, He simply did what He saw His Father doing and said what he heard His Father saying. He taught and lived the truth of His Father's will. He did not allow the injustice of His day to shape His ministry into a response of rebellion against Rome and its oppressive regime. Instead, He showed us that who we are and what we are called to do should shape our response to the things we encounter in this life.

Gentle: respectful of the feelings of others, considerate, mild, moderate, patient

To be considerate means that we count the cost of the effect our actions will have not only on ourselves, but also others. I am well aware that Jesus said we are to love Him more than family and friends, and sometimes we have to make difficult choices that influence our closest relationships. However, it is not the will of God that we wreck our families because we are seeking to live our dreams to the exclusion of caring for those we love.

This does not mean that we allow the feelings of our family members and friends to govern our lives. It does not mean that we are so dependent on their approval that we live in fear of displeasing them. At the same time, we must not run roughshod over them and become so calloused to their feelings that we "do the will of God" with no sense of the consequences to others.

Open to reason: not obstinate in clinging to one's opinion, listens

It is dangerous, especially in matters pertaining to the will of God, to forge ahead without being open to the ideas of others. We must always be open to reason. It is important for us not to be stubborn and self-willed.

In our human understanding, following God and obeying His will is not a "reasonable" thing to do. Who would sell all they have and give it to the poor? Who in their right mind would turn the other cheek? Who would give up a life of comfort and affluence to serve those in need? Who would sacrifice the security of a regular paycheck to follow God's calling? Nonetheless, we cannot use that principle as a pretext for forging ahead without considering the consequences or listening to the voice of others.

All of us are under some form of authority and account-ability. Even those of us who are ultimately submitted to the authority of God must also have some form of human accountability. This is good and necessary, and it keeps us from getting full of ourselves and going off on irresponsible tangents. We are dealing with what we believe to be ultimate truth from God Himself, and we have to be very careful how we handle it.

Full of mercy

Mercy is kindness or forgiveness shown especially to someone in a less powerful position. When making deci-sions, it is crucial that they be based in mercy. Mercy has two characteristics. It is first *active*. Mercy is more than just the absence of retaliation; it is showing active and inten-tional kindness. Secondly, mercy is not performed as a mere fulfillment of a command but is motivated by genuine inner compassion. Mercy is both a compassionate feeling of the heart and the action of extended kindness.

Righteousness must be bathed in mercy. E. Stanley Jones in his book *The Christ of the Mount* writes, "Righteousness unmoved by mercy is a hard, unlovely, Pharisaical, sour-visaged thing."[1]

Because we are all beneficiaries of God's mercy, we must learn to be less judgmental of others. James 2:13 warns us, "Judgment is without mercy to one who has shown no mercy" (NKJV). Those who give grace are those who never forget that they are products of God's infinite grace. They simply extend to others, in some small measure, the mercy that they themselves have received from the loving hand of God. Those to whom Jesus refers do not extend such mercy only on certain occasions, but they are "mercy-full." They, like Jesus Himself, are *full of mercy*. Compassion and kindness are not occasional responses but the pervasive quality of their lives. It is not mercy without backbone or accountability, but if it errs, it errs to the side of grace.

We experience the challenge of relating to others with mercy when we try to implement the truth of God in our lives and our society. It is often easier to know truth than it is to know how to apply it, and we can easily find ourselves making simplistic pronouncements of one extreme or another. First Corinthians 10:23 teaches us to seek a balance in this when it says, "'Everything is permissible'—but not everything is beneficial. 'Everything is permissible'—but not everything is constructive."

Impartial: without discrimination, partiality, or separation

God's will for us inevitably involves other people—family members, close friends, others who have a stake in the purposes of God. The way we walk out the will of God affects how we relate to other people, and the way we respond to other people affects how we see God's will. If we are swayed one way or another by how we perceive others and relate to them, our perception of God's will may be distorted. The wisdom of God is applied without regard to social standing, ethnicity, or political expediency.

It is easy to fall into the trap of making decisions involving other people on the basis of how they can best serve your own interests.

God loves people that you and I do not even like. If He is going to work through us, our hearts must be open to the love God has for all people.

I have experienced times when I was prone to give preferential treatment to certain people because of their notoriety or because of what they could do for me. Could they help me or be an asset to my ministry? Could their presence in our congregation boost our place in the community or add to our finances? If we have this kind of mind-set, the answer to these questions will determine how we relate to others. As James 2:2–4 teaches, showing favor to one necessarily means that we show disfavor to another.

Sincere: without hypocrisy or insincerity

James concludes his list of characteristics about godly wisdom with a reference to God's will for us to be sincere. We are to have unfeigned love that has at its roots both the mercy and truth of God. This is love that calls people out of destructive behavior patterns to a more excellent life. God is for people, not against them, and His love is profound and powerful. It heals and strengthens, builds up and does not tear down. It calls people out of sin and into a more excellent way so that they might become all that they were created to be.

Romans 12:9 states that "Love must be sincere." God does not love us for what He can get out of us, and neither should we use "love" as a manipulative tool to get our own way or to entice people to like us and support what we do. Genuine sincerity will flow through every part of our lives—who we are and the way we function—as an expression of the reality that we have been redeemed by the grace of God. The pres-

ence and power of Christ in our hearts should shine through
the goodness of our behavior, speech, and relationships. We
are not actors on a stage, trying to portray what we think a
Christian believer should look like. We live according to the
reality of who we are and who God is re-creating us to be.
We do not present a false appearance to those around us.
Our walk, our love, and our service must be honest, true,
and heartfelt. People today desire honest believers who are
real about their lives and candid about their shortcomings.

Applying Truth

As I mentioned earlier in this chapter, it is often easier to
know truth than it is to know how to apply it. Sometimes in
order to determine how to apply the truth, we are forced to
wrestle with it in great anguish. Those who maintain extreme
views in some ways have it easier than the rest of us. They do
not have to wrestle with issues or yearn to seek the perfect
will of God for people and situations. They simply spout their
extremist viewpoints. The rest of us discover the will of God
on our knees as we pursue Him and passionately cry out
for His direction. Genuine spiritual understanding does not
come easily. The soul that continuously and fervently seeks
after God's guidance will not always find itself in a place of
complete certainty, but it will rest in a place of blessing.

The ability to know God's purposes at any given time
will always arise out of the strength of our relationship with
the Lord. The closer we are to God, the better we can hear.
The more we are in tune with God's heart, the more we will
know and do His will. It is a function of devotion and obedience. There is no substitute for time spent communing daily

with God in worship and prayer. It involves seeking God's heart, listening, and then implementing what we know to be true in our daily lives. When we make mistakes, we learn from them.

We do not receive knowledge of the will of God the same way we obtain any other type of information. Rather, we receive it through spiritual revelation that God imparts to us by His Spirit and through His Word. Spirit-inspired knowledge proves itself to be the will of God as we walk it out in our daily lives.

Drawn, Not Driven

To be led by the Lord can be illustrated by an experience I had a few years ago while I was in Tanzania, East Africa, to speak at a pastor's conference. While I was there, the car in which I was traveling came upon a man who was driving a small herd of goats across the road with a homemade whip. As we drew near, we could see him whipping them madly and yelling at them to hurry up. It was a parabolic representation of the contrast between being driven toward something and being drawn to it.

Jesus called Himself the Good Shepherd (John 10:14). He is not behind us, whipping us into obedience and driving us forward in a hectic frenzy. He goes out *ahead* of His sheep, and they follow Him (John 10:4). Jesus is also called the pioneer of our faith (Heb. 12:2, RSV). A pioneer is the one who goes out ahead and makes the way for others. Our Lord is out ahead of us, inviting us to join Him where He already is.

Years ago, I was invited to participate in Bill Glass's national prison ministry. We gathered from all over the country at a particular location and then went into several prisons in the area to share Christ with the inmates. The first time I went into a maximum-security state penitentiary, I thought we were taking Jesus to the inmates. However, when I got inside, I found that Jesus was already there, living in the hearts and lives of many precious incarcerated brothers. We weren't taking Jesus into the prison at all. Rather, He was inviting us to join Him where He already was!

Some years later, I became involved in international missions. Mexico was the country where we first began to work. On our initial trip there, I thought we were taking Jesus to the people of Mexico. However, when I arrived there, I was once again in for a surprise. Jesus was already there, beckoning us to join Him in Mexico.

It is important for us to remember that we are driven by our lust, need, pride, or anger. But we are drawn by the Lord.

The will of God will never take us to a place where Jesus is not. Wherever His will takes us, regardless of what we find when we get there, we can be well assured that Jesus is already there. He simply invites us to meet Him there. The Lord is not behind us with a whip, driving us like that man with his goats. He is out ahead of us, inviting us to be with Him where He is—drawing us to Himself. In Jeremiah 31:3 God assures us, "I have loved you with an everlasting love; I have drawn you with loving-kindness."

Chapter 6

BASED ON UNCHANGING
FUNDAMENTALS

FOR MANY YEARS, my family and I have lived in Athens, Georgia, a city renowned for football. I have watched a lot of football—from the YMCA league for little boys to the professional level of the NFL—and I have noticed the obvious changes that occur as the players grow older, bigger, and stronger, and the offensive and defensive systems become increasingly more complex. However, *the basic fundamentals of the game remain the same.* For both the beginner and the experienced NFL veteran, football is all about being able to run, throw, pass, kick, block, and tackle.

At football practices, coaches drill their players in the nitty-gritty basics of the game. These drills are performed over and over until they become instinctual to each player. A portion of each practice is devoted to fundamentals because it is important to continuously work on them. Even the greatest players of the game never lose sight of them. They may get tired of the repetition, but oh the glory it brings!

As a licensed airplane pilot, I spent a lot of time learning the fundamentals of flight and the basic dynamics of aviation. Over the years, I transitioned from flying a basic, single-engine airplane to flying many different kinds of aircraft, including the Boeing 767 simulator. As I moved into the larger aircraft, the operating systems became more complex, but the basic principles of flying an airplane remained the same. Although I became increasingly more proficient and experienced as a pilot, I did not outgrow the need to do the fundamentals.

These are only two illustrations of the fact that learning and implementing the fundaments well, and continuing to do them well, are the primary factors in determining success or failure. The fundamentals make the difference in every endeavor of life. All the talent in the world will not make up for deficiency in this area. A talented athlete who lacks the fundamentals or refuses to continue to work on them will not reach his full potential and will eventually be beaten by the athlete who is more fundamentally sound. The team that is better at the fundamentals will win most of the time.

Lack of knowledge and ability in the rudiments of any undertaking will limit the degree to which one can progress in it. For instance, we can't expect to learn calculus if we do not know how to add or subtract. I wish I had learned the basics of typing and spelling, because my deficiency in these areas inhibits my ability to write.

The principle of learning and continuously practicing the fundamentals applies to the life of faith and walking in the will of God. We cannot expect to make spiritual progress if we are not willing to devote ourselves to the fundamentals of what it means to be a follower of Jesus Christ. We cannot advance to the higher levels of revelation if we are fundamentally unsound. If we try, our revelation will lack depth and maturity or we will simply fall. The fundamentals of the Christian faith never change, and they are the same at every level.

Mastering the fundamentals involves both knowledge and practice. We must know the important, basic principles and continuously live them out. There is no way around it, and there is no shortcut. A believer who has been well taught in the foundational principles of the faith knows them in the depth of his soul. Solid biblical and theological teaching does need not impede the work of the Spirit, and it can actually enhance the Spirit's power if it is not substituted for the work of the Spirit.

A person who is adept in biblical fundamentals and who is not entrenched in inflexible fundamentalism has the core of a solid believer. On the other hand, one who lacks the fundamental knowledge of the practice of the faith is always at a disadvantage. Thus, when someone comes to a saving relationship with Jesus Christ, it is essential that they be taught the fundamentals. This is not the same as imposing a certain religious perspective on them or indoctrinating them into a particular brand of Christianity. Instead, it means that we expose them to a solid biblical foundation of God's truth and then allow them the freedom to walk it out as God leads them.

There may some debate about what to include on a list of fundamental Christian truths. However, we may begin with the following:

- the nature of God
- the kingdom of God

- the plan of salvation
- the work of the Cross
- the Resurrection
- the lordship of Jesus Christ
- justification by faith
- the life of faith
- personal holiness
- service and mission
- worship
- Christian community
- prayer
- fasting
- healing
- love of others
- forgiveness
- charity
- justice
- the second coming of Christ
- the final judgment

Do you know what the Bible says about these fundamentals? How much do you know about them? How well do you apply them to your life and practice them? None of us understand or perform all of them perfectly, and we all need to improve. However, we can never take our eyes off them as we advance in our understanding of the nature of God and His will. In fact, being effective in the fundamentals of the faith is an essential component of God's will for us. We may progress to great heights of the revelation of God's glory, but the fundamentals of discipleship will always be relevant.

Discipleship

The basic framework of the Christian life is being a disciple of the Lord Jesus Christ. When Jesus walked the earth, He called individuals and said, "Follow Me" (Matt. 9:9, NKJV). That has never changed, and it remains true to this day. Following Jesus is essential to being a Christian. We were not called to be religious or to support a worthy cause. We were called to change the basic direction of our lives and begin to follow the King of kings and Lord of lords.

A disciple is one who learns, one who follows, and one who loves his teacher and wants to be just like Him. As disciples, we must study how Jesus lived and what He taught. We must follow His example and try to be more like Him in everything we do. Discipleship means that we do not confine ourselves to studying *about* Jesus, but that we seek to *know* Him, love Him, obey Him, abide in Him, and draw all our life from Him.

Jesus gave clear teaching about the meaning of discipleship. In John 15:4 He said, "Abide in me and I in you" (KJV). In John 15:8, He added, "Bear much fruit, and so prove to be my disciples" (RSV). He told us, "Abide in my love" (John 15:9, RSV), and clearly stated, "If you love me, you will keep my commandments" (John 14:15, RSV). As He spoke to a large crowd of people who had gathered to listen to Him, He asked, "Why do you call me, 'Lord, Lord,' and not do what I tell you?" (Luke 6:46, RSV).

If we claim to be a disciple, we must show it in the way we serve others. If we say we love Jesus, we must also express His love to others. Throughout history, every true disciple of Jesus Christ has given up claim to their own lives—they no

THE WILL OF GOD

longer live for themselves but for the One who died for them (2 Cor. 5:15). As we seek the will of God, it is simply not enough to know this objectively; we must give ourselves to follow Christ and live for Him.

Self-Denial

The practice of Christianity has changed with the advent of contemporary culture. Perhaps the greatest change I have personally witnessed is the growth of the consumer mentality in the North American church. This is the result of a fundamental shift in the way people approach the Christian faith and appropriate its teaching. In the past, the basic charge of Christianity was self-denial, the act of giving our lives in service to others. Today, however, the cost of following Christ has been removed, and Christianity is seen more as a means of having our own needs met.

This shift has happened as the baby boomers, children born to parents who lived through the trials of the Great Depression, enjoyed great prosperity in the decades following World War II. Baby boomers, along with their children and grandchildren, have come to believe that the world revolves around them. This mind-set of entitlement has, along with other factors, made us a headstrong and demanding nation. In the prosperity of our times, we have the luxury of unrestrained introspection, and we are, in fact, drowning in our self-absorption. Consumption is our nation's drug of choice, and shopping is our national pastime. We demand the best goods and services.

Because this consumerist mentality has found its way into the church, people no longer see the Christian faith as a call to self-denial and discipleship. Instead, they see it as a means of fulfilling their emotional and physical needs. They make huge demands for spiritual goods and services, and their emotional needs form the basis of much of the teaching. Local churches are under intense pressure to keep up with the demands of people for meaningful social activities, ministry for children and youth, and entertainment in worship services.

Christianity has always found itself in a tension between reaching out to hurting people and at the same time calling people to repentance and discipleship. Jesus clearly met people where they were. He performed most of His miracles out in the world, during His daily encounters with people. He healed the neediest people in society, and His love for them and the power He brought into their lives changed them physically, emotionally, spiritually, and relationally. Yet, the call of Jesus never changed: "Repent, for the kingdom of heaven is at hand" (Matt. 4:17, RSV). Modern discipleship should be no different.

Holiness

We are all called to holiness, for it is one of the fundamental precepts we can confidently identify as God's will for us. Holiness has two dimensions: (1) that we are separated and devoted to God, and (2) we are pure in our motives and behavior.

Separated and devoted to God

Exodus 30:26–29 lists the articles in the Old Testament tabernacle and tells how they were all anointed with sacred anointing oil. This was the process of consecration, by which everything in the tabernacle was made holy, dedicated exclusively for the Lord's service.

Everything—all the altars, tables, bowls, lavers, candles—was consecrated to God. A table might be quite an ordinary thing. However, if it was made for the service of God and consecrated for that purpose, its nature was dramatically changed. It was separated from the ordinary and devoted to God. It took on a special status and became holy, sacred. Because it was holy, it could not be used for ordinary purposes. Instead, it was treated with respect and dignity.

Exodus 29 describes how the priests also went through the process of consecration. They were washed with water and anointed with blood and oil. New clothing was placed on them. Then they presented themselves before God, dedicating themselves to His service.

Nothing is more wonderful than being cleansed from sin by the blood of Jesus, anointed by the oil of His Spirit, and presented before the Lord in dedication to His service. This is how we become holy to the Lord—consecrated to God, separated from temporal purposes, and devoted to His service. We do not have to be an ordained minister or priest. In fact, God has the same regard for all of us who have been made righteous by the blood of Jesus and not by our own merits.

As repentant, consecrated believers, we are no longer ordinary but holy to the Lord. No, we are not better than anyone else, nor should we act "holier than thou." But our lives have taken on special significance. We are sacred, and we must not take the holiness of who we are and demean or degrade it. We must not yoke ourselves with that which is unholy, for it would take what God has made so special and trash it.

I urge you to begin to see yourself as separated and devoted to the Lord. Treat yourself with as much respect as you would the sacred articles of the tabernacle. The concept of being holy is one of the greatest elevators of human dignity.

Pure in our hearts and actions

Holiness also relates to the way we think and live. It has been described as moral excellence, and it is a bedrock fundamental of God's calling for us. The psalmist David described two characteristics of holiness when he said:

> Who shall ascend the hill of the LORD? And who shall stand in his holy place? He who has clean hands and a pure heart.
>
> —Psalm 24:3–4, RSV

Having clean hands means that our actions glorify God, serve people, and are morally pure. God is displeased by the fact that many self-proclaimed Christians tell lies, cheat on business deals, do not pay their bills, and generally engage in a myriad of immoral activities. Such behaviors profane the name of the Lord and turn people away from the faith. They also cast a negative reflection on all who profess Christ.

A pure heart speaks of inner thoughts that are consistent with God's loving, righteous thoughts and are devoid of malice, envy, pride, lust, slander, and selfish ambition. God wants us to be holy both inside and out. Jesus severely condemned the practices of those who looked good on the outside but inside were empty, hollow, and full of all kinds of evil (Matt. 23:27).

It is the will of God that we exhibit holiness in the following ways:

- purity in our inner life (our thoughts and the intents of our heart)

- purity in our outer life (our actions and behavior)

- purity in our relationships with others

- love and fidelity to our family

- treating co-workers and employees with respect

- honesty and fairness in business

- seeking justice and equality for all people

- a lifestyle of integrity

Our way of life—our moral standard, the content of our heart, the way we live in public and private, the way we conduct business and treat other people—is a matter of vital importance. Personal holiness is the result of our cooperation with God's power. We can't walk in the honesty, integrity, and purity of holiness without the grace of God to help us; and He won't do it without our permission and participation. Holiness is both given as a precious gift of God and forged by obedience.

God's grace works together with our acts of surrender to Him and makes us holy by His power. Holiness is not the result of following a set of prescribed acts or rituals. Rather, it occurs because we are consecrated by God and made holy by the cleansing of the blood of Jesus, the washing of water by the Word, and the anointing of the Holy Spirit. First Corinthians 6:11 describes this work of God's grace when it says, "You were washed, you were sanctified, you were justified in the name of the Lord Jesus and in the Spirit of our God" (RSV). And 1 Thessalonians 5:23 adds, "May God himself, the God of peace, sanctify you through and through. May your whole spirit, soul and body be kept blameless at the coming of our Lord Jesus Christ."

At the same time, God can't make us holy against our will, and our personal involvement is vital. Second Peter 1:3–5 teaches that God "has given us everything we need for life and godliness" through His great promises. For this reason, we are to make every effort to add to our faith virtue, knowledge, self-control, godliness, brotherly affection, and love. In his letter to the Ephesians, the apostle Paul wrote, "I beg you to lead a life worthy of the calling to which you have been called" (Eph. 4:1, RSV). Hebrews 12:14 exhorts us to strive for "holiness, without which no one will see the Lord" (NKJV).

Living in holiness is a huge challenge because all of us constantly battle against the sin nature within us. Sin is like a ball and chain that we have to drag through life. In my struggles with the shame of unholy living, I finally decided I wanted to live in such a way that I had nothing to hide or fear. I wanted to be rid of the voice that told me I had no right to talk to God because of the things I had done. In my desire to be able to open my life completely to the scrutiny of God (Rom. 14:12; Matt. 25:19), I decided in my heart that I would seek to live so that my life would reflect the goodness and glory of the Lord. Every day, I have to work toward that goal. Sometimes, it can be a discouraging process.

Although we often fail, we must remember that God is gracious and we are made righteous by His grace, not our own efforts. Our failures should make us ever more diligent to grow in dependence on God's grace. Our honest recognition that we have sinned should make us less apt to be judgmental of the sins of others. None of us is immune. None of us are perfect. We are all guilty. I don't have time to judge the sin of others. I have enough challenge with my own

We seek to live holy lives not only because God has commanded it, but also because *it is the best way to live*. As believers, we are greatly influenced by the fact that we will stand before the seat judgment seat of Christ one day and give an account of our lives (Rom. 14:10). Yet, we also need to be convinced that it is best to live a holy life. This conviction will protect us from the danger of leading a secret life under the power of sin, and it will enable us to enjoy freedom in Christ.

Chapter 7

RECEIVING OUR INHERITANCE

S EVERAL YEARS AGO, I was praying in my study at home. It was at a time in my life when I was diligently seeking spiritual gifts. I wanted earnestly to see the glory of God. I wanted to see a demonstration of God's power. But that day God convicted me of wanting God's *things* more than I wanted *God*. Then God asked me a question that stunned me: *"If you lost everything, and still had Me, would it be enough for you?"* For a while I couldn't speak. What could I possibly say in response to that question?

With His question still reverberating in my heart, I opened my Bible and read the following verse:

> I consider everything a loss compared to the surpassing greatness of knowing Jesus Christ my Lord, for whose sake I have lost all things. I consider them rubbish, that I may gain Christ and be found in Him, not having a righteousness of my own that comes from the law, but that which is through faith in Christ—the righteousness that comes from God and is by faith.
>
> —Philippians 3:8–9

Many things changed for me that day. Not only did my perspective change, but my pursuits and desires changed dramatically as well. It wasn't that I no longer wanted the glory of God or God's power and gifts. However, more than anything else, I began to want God alone. I began to turn my heart to hunger after Christ so much that everything else in my life would pale in comparison to the surpassing greatness of gaining Him—being found in Him. I really wanted to get to the place where it would be enough if I lost everything and still had God. And I realized that there is a dramatic difference between my own righteousness and the righteousness that comes from God.

We often have to learn lessons more than once before they truly become part of who we are. A few years after the above encounter with God, I was praying about my future and the future of the church I was serving as pastor. It was an important season during which several endeavors were in the balance and I needed direction from the Lord. I was vehement as I prayed, "Lord, You have to move! You must do this! You must do that! Lord, go before me! Open the doors! Show me the way!"

On the surface, my prayer was decent enough. However, I was so caught up in the future and what I adamantly felt God needed to do, that I had taken my eyes off the precious present of my relationship with Christ. Oh how it must have sounded to the Lord for me to see Him only for what He was supposed to be doing for me.

Once again, God stunned my heart: "*Kent, I am your inheritance.*"

It was not a rebuke, but I sensed a certain degree of pain in the way God said it. It was spoken from the heart of God, who loved me deeply and intimately. Because I was so caught up in what the Lord was supposed to do for me, I had completely neglected the fact that my Christian life is all about my relationship with Him.

For the first time ever, I felt like I had to apologize to the Lord for hurting His feelings. He responded with the truth revealed in Psalm 16:5, "I am your portion and your cup" (author's paraphrase).

My heart spoke back to Him with sentiment from the same psalm, "You are my Lord. Apart from you, I have no good thing. You hold my future. My times and seasons are in your hand."

God is enough. Many faithful people had proclaimed this over the years, and now it was beginning to ring true in my own heart. I set my heart to experience the truth that God gives us every good thing: "He who did not spare His own Son, but gave Him up for us all—how will he not also, along with him, graciously give us all things?" (Rom. 8:32). God is a good Father and knows how to give good gifts to His children whom He loves (Matt. 7:11). He will direct our paths (Prov. 3:5–6). Our future is in His hands, and He will make a way where there is no way. God will fulfill all His plans for us. He will present us before His glorious presence without spot or blemish and with great joy (Jude 24, RSV).

Yes, God is our inheritance, our portion, and our cup— and that is quite enough! He reaches out to us like the father who not only welcomed his prodigal son home but also told the elder son, "You are always with me, and everything I have is yours" (Luke 15:31). We are talking about something more important than the gifts, power, or blessings God gives us. If we lost everything and still had God, would it be enough?

In the book, *God Is Enough*, Hannah Whitall Smith described a time when she encountered great difficulty and challenge in her life. She sought the counsel of a Christian friend. After she patiently let Hannah recount all the difficulties she was facing, her friend simply replied, "Yes, but then there is God."

Hannah was perplexed because her friend had nothing more to say. She thought that perhaps her friend may not have understood the complexity or depth of the difficulty, so she went back to her friend and again told her all that was happening in her life. Hannah's friend assured her that she indeed did understand her plight. She repeated, "Still, there is God."

Feeling very desperate about her struggles, Hannah did not give up but went to her friend again and again in hopes that she would understand her problem and provide some help. Perhaps she went with a degree of frustration, considering her friend's response to be no better than a trite religious platitude in the face of an infinitely more complex situation. However, her friend's response was always the same. She would compassionately tell Hannah, "I understand completely, but then there is God."

Hannah wrote, "At last, because she said it so often and seemed so sure, I began dimly to wonder whether God might really be enough, even for my need, overwhelming and peculiar as I felt it to be. From wondering, I came gradually to believing, that, being my Creator and Redeemer, He must be enough; and finally a conviction burst upon me that He really was enough, and my eyes were opened to the all-sufficiency of God."[1]

God is working to change the focus of my heart from what He can give me or do for me to seeking instead to be so united with Him and surrendered to Him that He can truly become my all-in-all. The result is a change in the way I serve God.

From Meaningful to Effectual to Worshipful

The will of God does not exist in a vacuum. If we want to function in it, we must be cognizant of the social, economic, political, and spiritual climate of our day. It is vitally important that we not only know the news of the world and be aware of the realities of the day, but that we also know the overall movements of the generations and the times and seasons in which we live.

People in my generation, commonly called the "baby boomers," generally consider it very important that our lives have meaning. One of our greatest fears is that we will live our lives without accomplishing something significant. We who are Christians often express our desire to "make a difference" through our service to God. William and Le Etta Benke, in their book, *Church Wake-Up Call*, write that Boomers are generally those who are, "Seeking meaning—Boomers appear to be searchers committed to finding a meaningful philosophy of life."[2] In contrast, the generations that have followed mine generally believe that life is not about something being meaningful, but all about relationships. In their book entitled, *Generation Driven Church*, the Benkes further state that "Boomers tend to be results oriented. They pursue goals, targets, and missions with vigor and enthusiasm. Xers have a different focus. What is important is relationships and experiencing acceptance and mutual caring of community."[3]

My generation will often respond to a scheduled activity by asking, "What are we going to do?" We want to determine if it is meaningful enough to warrant our participation. We each serve God out of our generational mind-set. This means that we who are baby boomers generally have to feel good about what we are doing. Our service for Christ has to be worthy of our time, resources, and effort. Generally speaking, it has to accomplish something significant. Regardless of our approach to ministry, selfishness is often woven into the fabric of our "selfless" service. We tend to operate with the same bottom line business mentality as the rest of the world. Instead of asking if our ministry pleases God, we tend to evaluate it almost exclusively by what we accomplish and if it meets our personal needs.

However, as I look at the life of Jesus, I am beginning to understand that we are not here to be served but to serve. God is calling us out of our self-oriented demand that our "service" has to be meaningful and effectual and to the place where true ministry unto the Lord asks the question, "Does it please the heart of the Father?" Accomplishing the Father's purposes is important, but we must ask ourselves something even more vital: Does what I do simply give God pleasure? Does it bring God glory? Is it worshipful?

Imagine doing something to the pleasure of the Father with such abandon that you give little thought of its personal significance or measurable outcome. Consider doing an act simply out of love and adoration for the Creator and Sustainer of all things. I am not saying that we should ignore the importance of effectiveness in ministry. However,

I am saying that our actions should no longer be governed exclusively by an exclusively pragmatic drive for results. For example, many of us when considering Jesus' command to "love your enemies" (Matt. 5:44) believe that if we obey that command, it will result in come kind of change in the life of the enemy. However, no such promise accompanies the command and we should not assume that it does. Perhaps it was intended to affect a change in us as we obey. Regardless, the point is we should obey because it is a command of our Lord, rather than first trying to gauge the odds of a "successful" outcome.

I am not advocating the mindless waste of God's gifts or of our time, talents, and resources. However, we must recognize the vast difference between the cold, calculated pragmatism of religion and the true passionate love of God from a heart that cherishes an act of worship above our perception of effectual service. We see this in John 12:1–8, which tells how Martha was serving a dinner in Jesus' honor at Bethany one day. As He was reclining at the table, Mary, Martha's sister, came and poured about a pint of very expensive perfume on His feet and then wiped His feet with her hair The fragrance of the perfume filled the whole house.

Judas Iscariot, who would betray Jesus, objected to this because he perceived the offering of her perfume as the waste of a valuable commodity. He expressed displeasure because the perfume, which was worth a year's wages, could have been sold and the proceeds given to the poor. He rejected her act of worship on the grounds that it was not effectual.

We see another picture of a worshipful heart in 2 Samuel 23:13–17. David was holed up with some of his mighty men in the cave of Adullam, and the Philistines were in control of Bethlehem. One day he verbally expressed his thirst for water from the well near the gate of Bethlehem. Three of his mighty men responded by breaking through the Philistine lines and drawing water from the well. When they brought it to David in the cave, he refused it and poured it out before the Lord.

Our practical minds are indignant at what appears to be a flaunting of religious excess after three of David's most valued men had risked their lives to bring him the water he desired. We are blinded by the pragmatism that keeps us from understanding something greater—worship—is happening here.

In the Old Testament, one of the vital aspects of tabernacle worship was the "libation," or drink offering. This was often a mixture of fine wine and oil, and it was simply poured out before the altar of the Lord (Exod. 29:38–41). Many of the offerings of the tabernacle were designed to accomplish something such as atonement for sin, purification of the articles of the tabernacle, or that of the priests. But the drink offering was designed simply to be a sacrifice to the Lord, an aroma well pleasing to God.

The apostle Paul testified that he was "already…poured out like a drink offering" (2 Tim. 4:6). As he looked back on his life and service to God, he did not recount his accomplishments or his effectiveness. Although he had accomplished much, he described his life as a libation that had been willingly poured out to God. His life was an act of worship that flowed from his desire to please the heart of God.

Will you join me in making this our passion and purpose?

Compelled to Commitment

When Paul wrote to the church at Ephesus, he called himself "the prisoner of Christ Jesus for you" (Eph. 3:1, NKJV). I believe this was more than a statement that he was incarcerated as a prisoner at Rome. Rather, he regarded himself as a prisoner of Christ Jesus Himself.

We may choose to live the Christian life for a number of worthy reasons, but Paul attributed his motivation to one thing: the love of Christ (2 Cor. 5:14). Imagine Christ's love for you and your love for Him being so compelling that it actually captivates your heart! This is what it means to become a willing "prisoner" for the Lord.

In Philippians 3:12, Paul further described the state of his heart by saying that he was seeking "to apprehend that for which also I am apprehended of Christ" (KJV). Imagine what it means to be *apprehended* by the love of Christ! Imagine that God's love is so real and so compelling that it has won your heart, captured your affection, and holds you fast. If this is true, our primary motivation will not be that which is meaningful or effectual, but that which is pleasing to the One we love, the One who loves us.

Several years ago my wife and I toured Greece and Turkey in the area of the Aegean Sea and went to such places as Thessaloniki, Philippi, Ephesus, and Corinth. We saw firsthand where Paul made his defense of the gospel and where he was beaten and thrown into prison. When Paul left these places, it seemed that he was undaunted, fully committed to the Lord Jesus, and anxious to go to the next place to share the unsearchable riches of Christ. What, except for the compelling love of Christ, could possibly motivate a human being to live with such commitment and devotion?

Captive to Commitment

The apostle Paul was not only compelled by the love of Christ, but he was also committed to willingly serve God as a minister to the Gentiles. This was God's calling for him, as revealed in Acts 9:15, "This man is my chosen instrument to carry my name before the Gentiles." As Paul walked out his commitment to this calling, he said in Ephesians 3:1, "I am a prisoner of Jesus Christ *for you*" (KJV, emphasis added).

When God calls us, His purpose is not that we will become religious, but rather that we will touch the lives of people on His behalf. To fulfill this divine purpose, we need the two ingredients of *calling* and *compassion*. We must acknowledge and walk in the calling of God, and we must also have hearts of compassion for the people to whom we are called.

If we lack the calling of God and serve others only because we have compassion, we will eventually burn out. The motivation of emotion alone will not sustain us. Regretfully, many pastors and missionaries who have been called to serve a specific group of people have lacked hearts of compassion. They have not really cared for the people God called them to serve. They are like the prophet Jonah, who was reluctant to obey God's call to warn the people of Nineveh about impending judgment. Even when he did obey, he had no compassion for the people.

Has God called you to give your life in service for someone who needs Christ? The church should be a place of healing and transformation. This can only happen if we who are in it will passionately desire to see God make a significant difference in the lives of the people in our communities. But we first have to love people. We have to hope that they open their hearts to Christ.

Serving as a pastor is sometimes very difficult. It sometimes involves relationships with difficult people and church meetings that are sometimes contentious. On more than one occasion, I have told myself, "That's it! I am done!" But the very next day, I have found myself back at it, doing my best to fulfill God's call to be a faithful pastor to the people He has given me to serve. Something happens when divine purpose meets the human heart. We become captive to commitment, a willing prisoner of those we serve.

A Sacred, Eternal Covenant

The concept of covenant, one of the most profound principles in the Bible, is the foundation of the reality of God's relationship with us. A covenant is not an agreement, arrangement, or contract. It is a binding relationship of love in which certain promises are made. It involves the firm commitment of two parties to each other. God relates to us in the context of the covenant we have with Him through Christ (Matt. 26:27–28). God is not only committed to us, He is committed to the covenant relationship He has established with us.

We can take great comfort in knowing this. Most of us ride a roller coaster of feeling close to God when we do well and distant from God when we do not. Some even believe that God loves them only when they are good. However, God's covenant with us is ever sure—He will always be faithful to it once we have entered into relationship with Him through faith in the blood of Christ. Even when we are unfaithful to the covenant, God is not unfaithful because He cannot deny Himself (2 Tim. 2:13, NKJV).

When a person swears an oath, he swears on something greater than himself. However, God had no one and nothing greater on which to swear, so "He swore by Himself" (Heb. 6:13, NKJV). Thus, God's commitment has been sealed by His solemn promise, and He cannot and will not deny it. Even if a person should stray from relationship with Christ, God remains faithful and awaits his or her return.

Abraham was convinced of God's faithfulness to His covenant. Romans 4:18–20 teaches that he was unwavering in his belief in God's ultimate, continuous commitment to him. As was the case in His relationship with Abraham, God has willingly bound Himself in love to us through a covenant relationship in Christ. God is all-powerful. He can do absolutely anything He wants, yet He has willingly bound Himself and limited His own freedom by entering into a covenant relationship with us. That is astounding!

Genesis 9:12–16 tells how God set a rainbow in the clouds as a reminder of the covenant He made with Noah that He would never again destroy all life on Earth with a flood. At Mount Sinai, God was so angry with the people of Israel that He was ready to do away with them and start all over with Moses. However, Moses reminded God of the sacred covenant He had made with Abraham, Isaac, and Jacob, and therefore God relented (Exod. 32:13–14). Having a relationship with God is not just about obeying the precepts of religion, but living in covenant relationship with the One who has made His solemn commitment to us in Christ. No doubt there are times when God is not happy with us. Perhaps there are even times when God is downright angry with us. However, God's commitment is not dependent upon His feelings for us at any given time

When I married my wife, Sandy, she and I stood before the altar of God and willingly gave ourselves to each other. We were free and self-determinate individuals, but we loved each other so much that we willingly bound ourselves in the sacred union of marriage. We were, and are, willingly captive to our covenant. I would never assume that Sandy always likes me. In fact, as in any marriage, we can occasionally be quite unhappy with each other. However, the strength of a marriage relationship is not found in exclusively in feelings for one another, but in the covenant made with each other. It is more than warm, happy feelings. It is our word, our bond.

This is the marriage covenant. God instituted it at the very beginning of Creation (Gen. 2:24) so that a man and a woman might live out the very kind of covenantal love He desires with us. For example, the promises of God are not applicable to everyone any more than a marriage vow is made to several people. The marriage vow is made to the betrothed—the one who is entering the sacred covenant of marriage. When we receive Christ as Savior and make Him Lord of our lives, we enter into the eternal covenant of "marriage" with God.

This is why the Bible refers to the church as the "Bride of Christ." As Christ's bride, we are assured of God's commitment to keep all His promises, and we become official heirs to all that He has. Each time we share in the body and blood of Christ, we are reminded of our sacred union with God.

"Then He took the cup, gave thanks and offered it to them saying, 'This is my blood of the covenant'" (Matt. 26:28). We draw comfort in knowing that the bond between ourselves and God is as irrevocable as His love for us. He will never forsake the word of the covenant ratified in the blood of His Son. It is up to you and me, therefore, to both enter that relationship and to be committed to it.

Chapter 8

BATTLING THE NEW SORCERY

I T IS VERY important that we discern the will of God and obey it. However, we must also be careful how we walk it out. We must beware of a counterfeit means of accomplishing the will of God. A counterfeit means of affecting the will of God uses force, control, manipulation, coercion, intimidation, seduction, and fear to institute the ways of God in individuals and in society. I believe these kinds of strategies constitute a modern, sophisticated, culturally adapted witchcraft as devilish as sorcery itself.

The Temptation of Jesus

It was a critical time for Jesus. He had not yet begun His public ministry, but He had a strong sense of who He was. He had a deep reverence for the Scriptures. Everything He understood to be true about life, God, and Himself arose from the sacred writings. He had been baptized, and that had been a glorious day. The heavens had opened, and the Spirit of God had descended on Him. A voice from heaven had made the pronouncement, "This is my beloved Son in whom I am well pleased" (Matt. 3:16–17, KJV). Baptism was a confirmation of who He was as the Son of God. Similarly, it is at our own baptisms that our identity as sons and daughters of God is confirmed.

Jesus knew who He was, but that was only half the equation. The other half was to determine what He was supposed to do with His life. Identity and purpose are joined. We need to know who we are and what we are supposed to do. This was the strength of Jesus, and it is our strength as well. Our strength is not in our gifts, talents, abilities, intellect, or looks. Our strength comes from knowing who we are as sons and daughters of God. That is why there is such a battle to confuse us of our identity—to make us unsure and insecure in who we are. This is especially true of young people in the critical years of establishing their own identity. It is vital that they come to know their place and purpose in God, the One who created them and loves them.

After He was baptized, Jesus went off alone to contemplate the course of His life and ministry. He wanted to discern the will of His Father, and He wanted to be exactly right. Jesus was not sent to do "any kind of good" available to Him. The will of God for Jesus, and for us, is more specific than that. Thus, He spent a long time alone praying and seeking God. He was yearning deep in His soul for the purposes of the Father to be revealed to Him. Some people are mildly interested in God's will for their lives, but for Jesus, it was His consuming passion. He prayed and He fasted.

It is interesting to note that during this time, Jesus faced an attack on His identity. The devil prefaced two of the temptations with these words, "*If you are the Son of God.*" (Matt. 4:3, 6, emphasis added). The words were an insidious attempt to undermine Jesus' confidence in who He was. As Jesus contemplated the course of His life and service to God, He was tempted to do three things that sounded good on the surface. After all, if it didn't sound good, it wouldn't be tempting, would it?

- *Turn stones to bread*—If Jesus did this, He could feed the world and eliminate hunger in an instant. This would be tempting, especially for someone who loves people. But Jesus said no. A ministry like that may be exactly what God wants for someone else, but it was not for Jesus.

- *Make a display of supernatural power by throwing Himself off the pinnacle of the temple at high noon, when the city is busiest. Angels would appear out of nowhere to rescue Him, and it will draw huge crowds*—What an opportunity for Jesus to reach people for God and gain their full attention! But Jesus knew that the kingdom of God is not putting on a show or creating a spectacle to attract a crowd.

- *Make Himself king*—Wow! That would really have been something. As the political king, He could have gotten a lot done. He could make the ways of God the law of the land. He could institute godly policies and put the nation on the right track. In fact, He could have the power to make Himself king over every kingdom and nation on Earth. There was just

one problem. To do it, He would have had to
bow down and worship the devil.

The pressure to be a national political leader would follow
Jesus as long as He lived on earth. Following the miraculous
feeding of the five thousand, Jesus perceived that the people
were about to take Him by force and make Him king, so
He withdrew to the hills by Himself (John 6:15). He did not
even take His disciples with Him. Perhaps they were under
the same hypnotic spell of power as the rest of the people.
When Jesus told His disciples that He was going to be killed
in Jerusalem, Simon Peter rebuked Him. He couldn't become
king if He was going to die! Jesus responded with the famous
words, "Get behind me, Satan" (Matt. 16:21–23).

Perhaps Judas Iscariot had the same nationalistic zeal as
many others. Perhaps he followed Jesus because it appeared
that He would be the long-awaited political leader who would
put an end to Roman occupation and re-establish Israel to the
international prominence it had under David's reign. Even
though he heard Jesus speak of suffering and dying to give
His life as a ransom for many, he either chose not to believe
Him or he just failed to understand. Those who are driven by
their own agenda or desire often fail to see anything to the
contrary. When it became apparent that Jesus was not going
to make a political move against the Romans, Judas' admira-
tion turned to hate, and Satan put it in his heart to betray
Him (John 13:27).

Even after all the dust of the crucifixion had settled and
Jesus had been gloriously raised from the dead, those who
followed Him still did not get it. Just before He ascended to
heaven, they asked Him, "Now? Will you do it now? Are you

going to finally restore the fortunes of our nation?" (Acts 1:6, author's paraphrase).

Jesus said no to the temptation to use force, coercion, intimidation, manipulation, and control to accomplish the will of God. The desire for power and the temptation to use force to institute the ways of God are so diametrically opposed to God that Jesus Himself called it satanic (Matt. 16:23). It is a natural tendency in all people who love God to want to see God's ways become pervasive in society. But somewhere we cross the line when we resort to certain manipulative measures to accomplish it. We are called to proclaim the kingdom of God by word and example, not to institute it by force.

The Nature of Sorcery

Sorcery is not benign. It has power, and it can accomplish things. It can create a spectacle that draws a crowd and amazes people. Sometimes, it can even elevate the person who practices it to an almost god-like status. Acts 8:9–11 introduces us to Simon, a man who practiced sorcery. He amazed people with the displays of his power, and they even called him "the divine power known as the Great Power." Perhaps he had learned it from his father or mother, or perhaps it was common to his culture. Whatever the source, it was not right.

Most people equate witchcraft with hexes and spells; curses and potions; vows and covenants; false gods; believing in lies; the worship of ancestors; the worship of the son, moon, stars, and the earth; and the worship of nature, superstition, objects, and idols. While many people blatantly practice the black arts, others have taken on a new sorcery that has adapted to the culture and the times. It is often quite subtle and insidious. Sorcery will always seek to imitate the power of God. It may even disguise itself as being in tune with God (2 Cor. 11:14).

An action is motivated either by a sincere desire to glorify God or is motivated to glorify a human being, institution, or ability. If an initiative is not grounded in the ways of God, it is sorcery just the same as outright witchcraft. The will of God is not just an end in itself; the means are just as important. We cannot legitimately accomplish the *purposes of God* by using any means other than *the ways of God*. We must turn away from all forms of control and manipulation and renounce its ways.

It is important that we guard against sorcery that manifests itself in the misuse of personal gifts we have received from God. Our personal abilities are marvelous gifts that we can release to God to glorify Him and accomplish His will. We can yield our intelligence, looks, charm, and natural abilities to God for His eternal purposes. And we can use our God-given creativity—the expression of His nature revealed at the very beginning of the Bible—to honor Him, the Creator.

However, we can also use the beautiful gifts God has given us as manipulative tools to influence people, promote ourselves, entice people to admire us, or simply to get our way. We can choose to exploit and debase our abilities to glorify the creature instead of our Creator. For instance, I have known people who have used their charm to gain the friendship of people. I have sometimes fallen into that trap myself. I have also seen people use their intelligence to never lose an argument. Some say they are glorifying God, but they are really only glorifying themselves.

In spite of the potential for misuse, our personal gifts and abilities can be a tremendous source of blessing. God gave them to us and delights when they are exercised in their God-given purposes. The key is to continuously submit them to God in humility, praying that they will be used for God's eternal purposes.

The Power of Intimidation

The power of intimidation is as the power of witchcraft, and it can make even the greatest people of God run for their lives. First Kings 19:1–4 illustrates this in the story of Elijah, who was threatened by Queen Jezebel and ran like a scared dog. He was ready not only to give up his ministry, but even to die. Many people have expressed paralyzing fear under the power of intimidation.

In my ministry as a pastor, I have been on the receiving end of intimidation and its venomous hiss. Like many people I have also been subject to the pressure of a "hard sell" sales tactic. You can literally feel the pressure. They can make you feel like you would be an idiot to pass up their deal. Jesus could not be intimidated because there was nothing anyone could take away from Him. He could not lose anything because He had already offered up everything He had to the Father. He wasn't trying to establish a constituency to support His ministry, and He wasn't running for office. He wasn't trying to protect His ego, and He wasn't trying to amass a fortune, protect an investment, or leave some personal legacy.

The only thing Jesus was adamant about was going to the cross. He set His face toward that end and would let nothing interfere because it was His Father's will. When Jesus' enemies could not successfully threaten Him with anything else, they threatened to take His life. However, they could not take even that from Him because He had already willingly laid it down (John 10:18).

Jesus had power to withstand intimidation not only because of His supernatural ability and divine knowledge, but also because He knew *who* He was and *whose* He was. In a similar way, we as believers may have spiritual gifts, abilities, talents, or theological knowledge. However, we can be strong against intimidation if we have security in our identity as God's children and know who we are and whose we are.

Fighting the Battle God's Way

As we live out the will of God, we are waging war against a spiritual enemy. We are in a spiritual battle against evil, and we need to understand the ways of the enemy and the strategies of the Lord. The forces that oppose the reign of Christ seek to confuse our identity and undermine the will of God in our lives. Thus, we must learn to fight the battle the Lord's way.

In 2 Corinthians 10:3–5 the apostle Paul gave us wise counsel for fighting the enemy: "Though we live in the world, we do not wage war as the world does. The weapons we fight with are not weapons of the world. On the contrary, they have divine power to demolish strongholds. We demolish arguments and every pretension that sets itself up against the knowledge of God, and we take captive every thought to make it obedient to Christ."

God has given us true spiritual authority in Christ so that we can affect change and advance His divine purposes. Through Christ, we have the ability to discern what is happening and how to respond properly. As long as we fight our battles the Lord's way and walk in proper spiritual authority, we prosper and are led from victory to victory. But if we forsake genuine spiritual authority and take matters into our own hands, we will begin to fight as the world does. We will resort to that which is nothing more than sorcery—force, guilt, intimidation, legalism, coercion, fear, embarrassment, and judgment—to impose our will.

Paul described the world's method of fighting as "disgraceful, underhanded ways" (2 Cor. 4:2, RSV). We must turn away from all counterfeit means of accomplishing what we believe to be the will of God. Our Savior refused to use control or coercion as a means of effecting His Father's will, and so must we.

Ecclesiastes 3:8 teaches that there is "a time for war and a time for peace." There is a time to fight, a time to go to battle. I am not trying to spiritualize everything, but we make a mistake if we fail to see situations from a spiritual perspective. We do wage war against a spiritual enemy, and we had better learn how to fight the battle the Lord's way. We must guard against being drawn into a battle on the enemy's terms and on his turf. This is what happens when the enemy starts the fight and we respond in kind. It is easy, when confronted by some kind of challenge, to respond with the same methods and ferocity. They get their lawyers, you get yours. They grab their guns, so do you. They form their coalitions, you form yours. You might actually win some battles. However, I learned a long time ago that we can't "out-wicked" the wicked. They are better at it than we are and have much more energy proceeding from anger and hatred than we do. Even if we win, we may forfeit the goodness of God in the process. The kingdom of God is entered by submission, repentance, and obedience. But "the violent take it by force" (Matt. 11:12). That is one reason we see so many examples of Christians hurting other Christians. Many believers are wounded by "friendly fire." The result is there are too often heinous acts done in the name of God. This is also why on one occasion where people opposed them, the disciples said to Jesus, "Lord, do you want us to command fire to come down from heaven and consume them?" But He turned and rebuked them, and said, "You do not know what manner of spirit you are of. For the Son of Man did not come to destroy men's lives, but to save them" (Luke 9:54–56, NKJV). This does not mean that Christians do not have to fight certain battles. It does not mean that God cannot call believers into the political arena. There may even be a time to take up arms to stop a relentless evil. Beware of your motivation as you go. Subtly, your heart can move from a sincere response to the call of God to the place where you are operating out of an entirely different motivation.

The Battleground in Our Hearts

The battleground exists not only in the world, but also in our hearts. A battle is being waged for our hearts, and this is why we experience so many assaults of fear and dread. It is the one reason we may sense heaviness in our hearts.

The battle is not about our spouse, our children, our boss, or our coworkers. It is a spiritual battle for the goodness of our souls. In John 10:10, Jesus said that Satan comes as a thief to "steal and kill and destroy." The evil one seeks to snatch up the precious seed of God from our souls. We must wake up to this reality.

If we do not understand the true nature of the battle and the strategies of the enemy, we will fight the wrong enemy in the wrong battle. People are not our enemy. As Ephesians 6:12 explains, "We wrestle not against flesh and blood, but against principalities, against powers, against the rulers of the darkness of this world, against spiritual wickedness in high places" (KJV). We are not out chasing ghosts, but we face a certain evil, whose intent is to use the situation at hand to confuse our identity, undermine our faith, make our love for Christ grow cold, and ruin our relationships.

The primary weapons of the enemy include fear, confusion, division, despair, and accusation. Lust, anger, pride, and greed are not just sins that incur the wrath of God, but they are places of vulnerability where the devil can get a foothold in us. We are fighting spiritual battles, and we must be careful that we do not to give in to malice, anger, bitterness, and revenge in our response to people who oppose us. In Matthew 5:44–45, Jesus said, "Love your enemies and pray for those who persecute you, that you may be sons of your Father in heaven."

Seeking the Strategy of God

David never went into battle without inquiring of the Lord, and neither should we. When David consulted God, He would almost always give him two very important pieces of information: the strategy and position of the enemy, and what his response should be.

Before we go charging into battle, we must know all that we possibly can about the situation we are facing. We don't get this kind of information in a one-time prayer session, but we must seek the Lord daily. As we watch and pray and wait, we will begin to see what is happening. We will be able to look above the fray and see the big picture. It might not be what we first think it is.

Sometimes, we will encounter evil as a full frontal assault that is easily recognizable. Most of the time, however, evil is subtle, and the enemy may try to divert our attention to one area so he can make an insidious attack in another. For example, our children do not get hooked on drugs because some evil-looking guy forces them to become addicted. If that were the case, it would be easier for them to just say no. Most of the time, however, it happens because they are at a party having a good time with their friends when out of nowhere someone hands them something and they drink, smoke, or swallow it. Thus, the destructive addiction begins.

The enemy's ploys are endless and sinister. If he cannot entice us to sin, he will attack us in other ways. He will overwhelm us with busy-ness, even seemingly godly pursuits. Or he will send someone into our fellowship to create division or theological confusion. He often comes disguised as an angel of light, a wolf in sheep's clothing. As Paul said, "We are not unaware of his schemes" (2 Cor. 2:11).

As we ponder the challenges in our lives—in our marriages, with our children, in our churches, or at our jobs—we must seek the counsel of the Lord: What is really happening? What is the real issue? What is the nature of the battle, and what exactly is at stake? We must not go off half-cocked or react from our flesh. Instead, we must wait, watch, and pray. The Lord will bring revelation, and we, by godly wisdom, will begin to see what God sees. This can only happen in an atmosphere of humility and genuine love.

When we have a true understanding of the battle before us, we must determine what God wants us to do about it. It is our natural tendency to take matters into our own hands, seize control of the situation and try to fix it according to our own understanding. However, if you wait, watch, and pray, God will give us a specific strategy for each situation. He will not resign us to a response of impotent inactivity or a boorish display of the power. Rather, He will guide and enable us to respond with true spiritual wisdom that implements genuine spiritual authority.

Chapter 9

REVEALED IN WORSHIP

NOT LONG AGO, a friend was telling me about the challenges of working for a large corporation. The most frustrating aspect of his job was that he never really knew where he stood with his division manager, the person to whom he directly reported. He was frustrated because he was uncertain about what was expected of him and how well he was doing. "He and I never meet," he exclaimed. "I think my manager feels like everything I need to know is in the corporate manual and my personnel job description. That's not enough for me. I need face-to-face guidance and feedback."

God wants to meet with you. Sure, He has given us the Bible, our complete manual for truth and the job description for us as believers. However, we still need more. No, we do not need another manual, another book, or a better job description. We are confident that the Bible contains everything we need to know. We need to meet with God and have relationship with Him. God knows this, and He reveals His loving presence and will to us as we meet with Him in the place of worship.

In Exodus 25–31, God gave Moses the plan for building the tabernacle, where He promised to meet with the people of Israel. It can be a bit tedious to read these chapters because of their detailed instructions concerning laws, priests, offerings, and the work of making the tabernacle and all its plates, bowls, and altars! Even the best-intentioned of us sometimes find it difficult to wade through the material in this part of the Bible. Yet, it can actually be a rich source of the precious truth that God desires to meet with us.

As I was reading the book of Exodus one day, Exodus 25:22 caught my eye. In the midst of all His instructions about tents and altars, God said, "There, above the cover between the two cherubim that are over the ark of the Testimony, *I will meet with you*" (NIV, emphasis added). He was telling us that He wants to meet with us.

God Offers to Meet With Us

I vividly remember the first time I went to Africa. It was in Tanzania, East Africa. While I was there I met with a group of Christians for a worship service. I loved it, but it was all so new to me. The people spoke and sang in Swahili, a language I did not understand. Since I had no idea what was going on, I just watched the people around me and tried to do what they did.

As I learned about the dynamics of African worship, I began to think about worship itself. For years I never really gave the attention to worship that I should have. Like most people, I just did it. My view of worship was that God is God and we are, of course, supposed to worship Him. God is great and we are supposed to praise Him. I reasoned that the manner in which we did that was a function of our upbringing, our temperament, our personality, or our culture.

And then I read God's words: "I will meet with you" (Ex. 25:22). When I did, I began to recognize that worship is not just something God requires of us, it is something He offers us. *Everything will change in our relationship with God and with our very lives if we can begin to see worship as an opportunity to meet with God.* This applies to what we normally consider worship—the corporate expression we call "going to church." It also applies to our individual times of worship and prayer, which we may identify as our personal prayer time, devotions, or quiet time.

Imagine what would happen if we begin to think of going to church as going to meet with God. Or consider the change that would occur if we replaced the words "I am going to do my devotions" with "I am going to meet with God." These changes would reflect the fact that worship is not just another ritual in a long list of religious requirements. It is so much more than people simply giving God the praise to which He is entitled. God's purposes in worship extend far beyond the fulfillment of a religious obligation.

Worship was given to us, not required of us. It is a precious gift of God by which He brings us into closer relationship with Him, releases His divine purposes in us, and forms us into all that we were created to be. It is a pattern of meeting with God so that we can become His dwelling place.

I have always wanted a deep and rich prayer life. At times, I would force myself to do it regularly. Sometimes I would succeed for a brief season. However, I could never really reach the point where it became a part of my life. This changed dramatically when I began to see my prayer times not so much as a spiritual necessity but as opportunities to meet with God. I stopped feeling like I *had* to pray and began to see it as a *privilege* God had given me. I actually began to look forward to meeting with God, and soon it became a real desire of my heart. I made sure that I built it into the schedule of my day. I even began to consider in advance the things I wanted to talk with Him about. Soon, I would also learn that God had things He wanted to present to me as well—things He wanted to talk to me about, and things He wanted to do in me.

God Gives Us His Commands

As long as we see worship as a requirement, it will be difficult to become excited about it. Even if we consider it a time to meet with God, it will hold little appeal if we believe God is just going to tell us more things we have to do. What if God had said, "There I will meet with you and give you everything you need to live?" Our attitude and practice of worship will change dramatically when we begin to realize that God has something He wants to give us.

God gives us His commands, not to place harsh requirements on us, but for our blessing and prosperity. They are an internal work of the grace of God that is manifested by a change of heart, mind, and behavior. As long as we view the laws and commandments of God as external requirements that are imposed on us, they will be nothing more than instruments of death. They will become an unattainable standard that will eventually lead us to resent the One who gave them. We cannot expect to obey God at gunpoint.

"Obey or else" doesn't work. In the long run, it just produces frustration and resentment.

All this, of course, is predicated upon the premise that we want to obey God. Obedience begins with love for God and the belief that His ways are just and right and good. David's heart was disposed to love God in that manner. David expressed it when he prayed, "Lead me in the path of thy commandments, for I delight in it" (Ps. 119:35, RSV). Twelve verses later he repeated his testimony, "I find my delight in thy commandments, which I love" (v. 47, RSV). The apostle Paul testified, "The law is holy, and the commandment is holy, righteous and good" (Rom. 7:12).

Worship is the means through which the righteous laws of God are fashioned within us. It is not just a one-way-street whereby we come and give praise and offerings to God. Rather, it is meeting with God so that His will can be formed and released in us. Through worship, the life of God flows in us. He works in us so that His commands are no longer something we have to do but something we get to do. Even so, it is more than God giving us commands.

The Place of Worship

The place of worship is not a physical location, but a spiritual position outlined in Exodus 25:22: it is "above the cover between the two cherubim that are over the ark of the Testimony."

Above the cover

The cover, which was called the "mercy seat," represents the mercy of God poured out in Christ. It is the place of atonement. It never ceases to amaze me that centuries before Christ came to live as a human being God had laid the foundation for Christ's atonement. It was built into the pattern of the tabernacle. When we stand in the presence of God, we are not there because of our own innate goodness, but by the mercy of God in Jesus Christ. I wonder if you have ever been in worship, or trying to pray, and something sinister whispered in your ear, "You don't belong here. You know what you've done. You have your nerve trying to pretend you are a faithful believer in God!" Actually, that would be true—except for the fact that our right to be in the presence of God is not based on what we have done but on the mercy of Christ.

The place where we stand in the presence of God is not one based on our own merit, but on the atoning grace of God through Jesus Christ. This is what most assuredly gives us the right to be there. Through Him we have access to "this grace in which we now stand" (Rom. 5:2).

Between the two cherubim

The cherubim are the winged creatures that inhabit the royal heavenly court of God. They are always in God's presence, and they represent the spiritual realm in which God dwells. Therefore, when we worship, we transcend the earthly plane of physical space and time and enter the greater spiritual reality that is always around us. As we become more experienced in worship and in opening ourselves to divine reality, we will experience a more profound sense of transcending the temporal space and time of Earth and entering into the heavenly realm.

Over the ark of the testimony

The ark of the testimony was the ornate box that contained the tablets upon which the commandments of God were written. It represents the covenant of God, the living relationship between God and ourselves through which God's promises become applicable to us. The foundation that undergirds our worship is God's unwavering commitment to us through Jesus Christ. Therefore, our worthiness in the presence of God does not ebb and flow with our daily behavior or variance of our immediate feelings. It remains constant in the unchanging affirmation of His covenant.

The Pattern for Worship

We receive worship as a gift from God, but the pattern for worship does not have its origin in our personal preferences or traditions. *Unless and until we worship in accordance with the pattern God has given us, it will never serve its true purpose.*

Most of us give little or no thought to our worship. While we may plan our church services to a degree, we often fail to ask essential questions about the pattern God has established for worship. Why do we do what we do? What do we hope to accomplish? How does God want us to worship? In the American church, current worship patterns are, for the most part, the result of 1940s tradition or the more contemporary style that began in the 1960s and 1970s. We often develop our theology to fit our worship pattern instead of following a pattern that is based on what God has set forth in Scripture.

Worship can have a variety of expressions, and they need not be categorized as traditional or contemporary, reverent or Spirit-filled. God's pattern for worship involves order. It is not chaotic, mindless, or filled with inappropriate expressions of zeal; neither is it under the dictatorship of an artificially imposed tradition. What is commonly called reverence is really an imposed standard of behavior. True reverence is a response to the glorious and holy presence of the Almighty. Making plans for worship does not necessarily thwart the movement of the Spirit, but it is important that we allow Him to lead it.

In a similar way, we as individual Christians should have a pattern or structure for our devotional times. I am not advocating rigidity; however, I am saying that we should think about what we are doing and why we are doing it in our times of personal prayer. Meeting with God should be important enough that we do it with a sense of order that reflects our sincere intention to grow in our relationship with Him.

In John 4:23, Jesus laid a foundation for our understanding of all worship when He said, "A time is coming and has now come when the true worshipers will worship the Father in spirit and truth." He showed that the pattern for worship is based on the truth of God's Word and has the life of the Spirit. It is a biblical pattern that is characterized by life and freedom that God, the Holy Spirit, brings. Through God's Spirit, miracles will be performed and people will be transformed. However, the life of the Spirit should never be confused with a particular style of worship.

Certain principles or building blocks should be in place each time we meet with God. In the remainder of this chapter and also in the next, I would like to present these building blocks, which, I believe, follow a biblical pattern.

Preparation

Whether we are walking in the door of the church or into our place of personal prayer, we cannot expect to instantly turn off the world and immediately focus our attention on entering the presence of the Lord. For instance I am amazed sometimes at how a family can be transformed from their car to the door of the church. The car screeches to a halt in its parking place, the doors fly open, the parents and children jump out, the dad is yelling at them like a mad man to quit fighting and get into church. By the time they reach the door, they look like the perfect, contented family! There has been a miracle transformation already!

I meet with God for personal worship and prayer in my home study. God's presence seems to linger there, and it has become a very special place for me. However, when I sit down in my chair, my mind is often on many other things. When I have just walked in and am still carrying the cares of my daily life; it takes some time to prepare myself to worship and pray. I have to shed my thoughts about the "stuff" of the world and begin to focus on God.

As I begin with time in the Word, my mind must begin to shift from my previous activities to the wisdom of the kingdom. I also have some devotion books that I read, but I always allow them to lead me into the Bible. I want to read the Bible more than I read anything else. I will read a chapter or two from one section of God's Word and see where that might lead me. I also read a psalm, and this usually leads me into praise, the doorway to His presence. I try not to do the same things all the time so that these meetings with God do not become monotonous. I share this simply as a suggestion so that you can begin to set up your own method for meeting with God.

Consecration

The tabernacle had two important articles at the entrance to the tent of meeting. One was a basin in which those who entered the presence of the Lord would be washed with water. The second was the altar where the blood of the sacrifices flowed. As we prepare to enter the time of meeting, we ask the Lord Jesus, our great High Priest, to come, take pure water, and wash us thoroughly. We then ask Him to forgive our sins and apply His precious blood to us—body, mind, and spirit. We ask Him to strip away the filthy rags of our misdeeds and replace them with "fine linen, bright and clean" (Rev. 19:8).

After we have done these things, we can enter the tabernacle of the Lord's presence as priests consecrated to the Lord's service. We minister before God not only for ourselves, but also on behalf of everyone He has put on our hearts and everyone we serve. We are, as 1 Peter 2:9 says, a kingdom of priests and a holy nation. I try to be mindful of this consecration and sacred privilege every time I enter the place of meeting.

In our individual devotional times, it is important that we be prepared spiritually, mentally, and physically to worship the Lord God. In the corporate setting, we and our worship leaders should be similarly prepared, cleansed, anointed, and consecrated.

Expectation

We ought to have an eager excitement about meeting with God, a prevailing sense of expectation that He is going to do something wonderful. Too often, however, our meeting times with God are characterized by a sense of obligation or boredom with little regard for the One with whom we are privileged to meet.

Let's imagine that you and I had set up a time and place to meet. However, I arrive late and obviously have my mind on other things. I constantly look at my watch, and I don't really listen to you. I generally give the appearance that I would rather be somewhere else. I wonder if this at all characterizes your meeting times with God. Unfortunately, too many churches do not conduct worship in ways that foster anticipation and passionate involvement.

Invocation

An invocation simply means a prayer to invoke or invite God to come and meet with us. Whether we are alone in prayer or in the presence of other believers, each person who worships God should begin by saying, "Lord, I invite you to come. I desire your presence here." There is no formula for invoking the presence of the Lord. God inhabits the praise of His people, where Jesus is exalted and honored, and where God is welcomed and desired. Our simple prayer of invitation uttered in faith can be, "Come, Lord Jesus."

Exaltation

The acknowledgement and exaltation of the Lord Jesus Christ is at the core of worship, and it changes the spiritual climate of the place where we meet with God. Therefore, it should not surprise us that Psalm 100:4 exhorts us to enter the gates of God's presence "with thanksgiving and his courts with praise."

We praise God because He is worthy of praise. He is highly exalted and a great and mighty God. Therefore, we do well to begin our prayers with a time of praise and adoration for the Lord. Let us lift up His name and speak aloud of His excellent greatness. God will be pleased if we ask His Spirit to release words or a song that will glorify Him. Instead of relying only on written words, we can praise God in our own words. We can't get it wrong, for God will be exalted. He is not judging our articulation.

Participation

In John 12:32, Jesus said that when He is lifted up, He will draw all people unto Himself. Thus, as we exalt Christ in worship, we not only usher in the presence of God, but we also invite others to enter into His presence. To enter in, we must first come into His presence and then participate fully. Sadly, worship is primarily a cerebral exercise for most people in the modern church, and anything beyond intellectual involvement is regarded as emotionalism. In far too many cases, the various aspects of worship only serve as preparation for the sermon.

We are missing the point! Worship is the vehicle of the Spirit's release. In worship, the power of God is released for salvation, healing, revelation, transformation, and empowerment. The teaching of the Word is an important part of the Spirit's ministry, but only a part. Let us participate fully in our times of corporate worship and abandon ourselves to the Lord so that we might receive all that He has for us and become all that He has created us to be.

Worship only accomplishes its purposes if we engage in it with all our body, mind, and spirit. If we are distracted with things of this life, it will be difficult—if not impossible—to fully enter into God's presence. If we are worried about our image or what others will think, it will limit what we can experience of God's glory and what He can accomplish in us. Worship, like the Christian faith itself, is a corporate venture; you cannot worship properly without engaging others at some level. We do not worship God alone.

Manifestation: God's Presence in Worship

As we fully participate in worship, we can expect God to come with a glorious manifestation of His presence. We see a glorious example of this in 1 Kings 8:10–11, which describes what happened when the temple was consecrated in the time of Solomon:

> The priests withdrew from the Holy Place, [and] the cloud filled the temple of the LORD. And the priests could not perform their service because of the cloud, for the glory of the LORD filled his temple.

This must be our foremost desire—that God will manifest His presence—when we meet corporately as the church or have our private times of devotion. God is not some

mysterious cosmic force, but our loving Father who desires
to be known by us. We do not worship an unknown God,
but as Jesus said in John 4:22, "We worship what we do
know." Our hope is that God will come and inhabit the
place where we are.

As Exodus 25:22 says, the place where God meets with
us is *above* the mercy seat, *over* the ark of the testimony,
between the wings of the cherubim. God comes down to the
place where we are, but we also *rise up* in our spirits to meet
with God. This truth is reflected in the traditional opening to
the service of Holy Communion when the leader says, "Lift
up your hearts," and the people respond, "We lift them up to
the Lord."[1]

What does it mean to "lift up your hearts" to the Lord?
Each of us, to a large degree, has control of our spirit. The
mind and the spirit work together in such a way that we each
can make a conscious choice to lift our spirit to the Lord and
come into His presence. It is important that we cultivate this
ability to lift ourselves to the spiritual plane where we can
meet with God and then commune with Him in our spirit,
mind, and body.

The place of worship is an elevated position. In a sense,
we rise above the mundane confines of the present world and,
for those few moments, see life through the eyes of eternity.
Seeing life from God's perspective puts all things in a new
light. Perhaps some things that deeply trouble us can be seen
as temporary. Our anxious spirits can be put to rest when
we see that our lives here and now are but a small portion of
our eternal existence. We must understand that our personal
salvation cannot be disassociated from its greater context of
what God is doing in all of creation. It is the Grand Story of

God—from alpha to omega—from the beginning to the end. Through our personal faith in Christ, we are doing more than simply receiving forgiveness of sins and a reconciled relationship with God. We are actively participating in that Grand Story. We are entering into the saga, becoming part of its flow, and being renewed in the hope of being restored with all of creation. This can only be seen through the perspective of eternity.

We must learn to cultivate an awareness of God's presence. It often takes time for the Lord's powerful, loving presence to come, but He will come. If we are in a church where Jesus is honored and His presence is welcomed, He will come. If we are alone in the place of prayer, seeking God with all our heart and waiting on God, He will come. Worship is more than simply listening to a sermon and having something to think about. It is an encounter with the experiential reality of the Almighty.

Sometimes God's presence comes as an awesome power that can literally take our breath away. It elicits a response of reverence that is not a forced silence, but a natural reaction to the holiness and love of God. Other times the presence of God is so sweet, so incredibly loving, that it can bring tears to our eyes. It is not the same every time. Sometimes it is more manifest, and other times it comes in waves. If we continue to wait, the Lord will often come again and again. The will of God is revealed in the context of worship and prayer.

Chapter 10

RELEASED THROUGH WORSHIP

MANY PEOPLE MAKE the mistake of believing that the feeling of God's presence—our emotional "chill bumps"—is the end-all purpose of our meetings with Him. However, the coming of the presence of God does not signal the end of the encounter, but the time when the real business begins. God wants to accomplish so much in our meetings, and we must, in solemn communion, give Him the opportunity to work in our lives. As we meet with God in worship, we can expect Him to transform us into all that He created us to be.

Formation by God

The purpose of worship is not simply to glorify God, who is certainly worthy of our praise. Worship is given to us by God as a means by which we can be transformed into all that God created us to be. It is in the place of worship that we are formed into the people God calls, "a holy nation" (1 Pet. 2:9). It is through individual and corporate worship that God's life is formed within us, we get our "marching orders" and we are released for the purposes of God.

Formed as the people of God

When we are in the presence of God, we are formed by the power of the Holy Spirit. This may be an immediate and powerful change, or it may be more of a process. As we meet regularly with God, we will experience a gradual but definite change in our hearts and our thoughts. Ultimately, it will manifest itself in changes in our behavior as individual believers.

We are not only formed as individuals, but we are also formed in the context of our life with other believers. We are formed as the people of God, a holy nation, the fellowship of the living God. This is why our participation in corporate worship is critical. We are not to be lone rangers, worshiping in individual isolation.

In the living organism of the church, called the body of Christ, we do not belong only to ourselves. We belong to the family of believers. God has given certain revelation of Himself that we cannot receive on an individual basis, but only in the corporate setting of the church. He is not just forming a bunch of individuals, but a *people* He calls His own. This does not make us superior to anyone, nor does it give us any greater entitlement. In fact, it gives us a greater obligation to live worthy of the calling to which we have been called! (Eph. 4:1, NKJV).

Becoming disciples

Jesus placed a high priority on making disciples when He gave us the great commission in Matthew 28:19–20.

Discipleship is certainly a function of training, education, and practice, but it is also a vital purpose of worship. Our time with God should not make us "holier than thou." Instead, it should give bring us to a more profound reverence for God, a deeper humility, and a greater desire to serve people. Our time with God should not make us seem inappropriately spiritual, but it should definitely increase our ability to positively influence the people we come into contact with each day.

Being built up as Christ's body

Our participation in corporate worship is vital and necessary. We, as individual believers, are limited in what we can do on our own, and we will eventually drown in our own thinking if we are isolated. However, it is not simply our limitation which should prompt us to join ourselves with the faith and life of others. Christian faith is social and communal in its very essence. In other words, Christianity is a team sport. Being part of a healthy, balanced, vibrant community of faith brings us wholeness as individuals and will keep us from going off on our own tangents, without the input and accountability of others. It will help us discern and walk in wisdom and the will of God.

This kind of ministry can happen because, as 1 Corinthians 12:7 teaches, God has given spiritual gifts to the church for the common good. He is working to build up or edify the church. He does this through the ministry of several spiritual gifts, including wisdom, knowledge, faith, healing, miracles, prophesy, and tongues. Ephesians 4:11–13 further explains that God has given the church apostles, prophets, evangelists, pastors and teachers to prepare us for service so that we may be equipped to serve, grow in unity, move us toward maturity, and be formed into the likeness of Christ.

Impartation From God

When we think of worship, we probably consider it as saying prayers, singing songs, making offerings, and hearing sermons. However, it is very important that we see it as an exchange of life with God in which we share our lives with Him as He imparts His life to us. Most of all, through the impartation of His nature and character, God shapes and molds us into the likeness of Christ.

What does God think?

We have access to the deep things of God's heart through the Spirit. As we meet with God and commune with Him by the Spirit and in the Word, we begin to have a growing sense of His perspective on things. This is why it is so vital to take everything—every hurt, every challenge, and every issue—to the Lord first. We need to have His perspective before we make any judgments of our own.

If we are faithful to meet with God, over the course of time our hearts and minds will be molded by the Spirit and Word. A godly perspective will replace our earthly, carnal viewpoint, and we will have what 1 Corinthians 2:16 calls the "mind of Christ." Remember, this knowledge will not be perfect, and we must always consider things in the context of the faith community. However, we can walk and live with a measure of confidence that we have the mind of Christ concerning ourselves, other people and the world.

How does God see you? We may see ourselves very differently than He does. How does God see the people around us, and how does He want us to view them? What is God's heart for our families, our churches, and our cities? Without the influence of God, you and I will inevitably see things through the flawed filter of our own distorted and prejudiced perspectives.

What does God think about the situations we face with our families, our jobs, our finances, or health? I am not talking about simply taking a scripture or two and frantically praying for God to help us. I am talking about entering the presence of the Almighty to seek His divine perspective on the real nature of the challenge and the response we should make to it. It takes time to bring your heart and mind into alignment with the perspective of God. It cannot be hastened. Few people are patient enough to seek God and wait as the perspective of God is revealed and formed in them. Often, I will sense in my heart that God is guiding me to respond in a particular way to a given situation. However, I am not ready to carry out that response until my heart is also aligned with the heart of God. Otherwise, I may proceed with the right action, but my motivation will be all wrong—it may be carnal, selfish, or angry. God's heart, however, is always disposed to seek redemption and reconciliation.

Our perspective on the world can be easily swayed by the voices around us. We are inundated daily by political opinion and reactionary rhetoric. It is better if we rise above the din and seek to apprehend a worldview based in the heart and purposes of God. As we do, we will receive the impartation of His great love which He revealed to the world when He gave His only Son (John 3:16).

What are God's plans?

God's will for our lives is part of a greater whole. His plans for us do not exist in isolation. Rather, they are an integral part of His plan for the whole world. When we enter the life of faith in the Son of God, we are participating in something God began before time and will bring to glorious consummation in the Day of Christ. As chaotic as this world seems, it is not governed by chance or fate. God's eternal will—that which He has written and spoken—will indeed come to pass. Not one word that God has spoken will fall to the ground until all is fulfilled (Matt. 5:18).

We can learn a great deal about God's plan for the world simply by reading what He has spoken in the Word. When Jesus' disciples asked Him about the end of the age and His glorious second coming, the first words out of His mouth were, "Watch out that no one deceives you" (Matt. 24:4). He also said in Matthew 24:6 that we should not be alarmed by world events. We can expect things to unfold exactly as God has said in His Word.

Jeremiah 29:11 promises that God's plans for us are for our good, to prosper us and not to harm us, to give us a future and a hope. Because God weaves His will for our lives into the fabric of His prevailing will for humanity as a whole, we must see His will for us in that context. It is marvelous that God loves us. It is even more incredible that God can simultaneously direct our individual lives and use them in accordance with His ultimate will for the whole world. What we do is important because it is part of an integrated, larger whole.

This does not mean that God's plans for us are written in stone and cannot be altered. We can choose the level to which we will participate in God's plan. We can determine if we will work with Him or fight against Him. When Israel was in the wilderness, it was clear that the nation was going to Canaan's Promised Land. That was the irrevocable will of God. However, each individual in Israel chose if they would set foot on the soil of Canaan. A whole generation of Israelites did not enter the land because they hardened their hearts and refused to believe Him (Ps. 95:10). This is all the more reason for us to obediently attune our hearts, minds, souls, and bodies to the will of God!

Participating in the divine nature

Let me share with you an important Bible verse. It is 2 Peter 1:4: "Through these, He has given us His very great and precious promises, so that through them you may participate in the divine nature and escape the corruption in the world caused by evil desires." It is not possible to begin to unlock all of the depth of what is being said here. Rather, I want to call your attention to the phrase, "participate in the divine nature." If you were to study the word *participate* you could perhaps consult *Strong's Exhaustive Concordance of the Bible*, and it would tell you that the word is translated from a Greek word, *koinoneo*, which basically means to enter into fellowship with, to become an associate or partner. It is a word often referred to in the church as the shared life of Christian fellowship.

When the Bible uses the concept of *fellowship*, it speaks of something much deeper than simply being together to have a good time. It means sharing life together. This is not a superficial sharing of life. It is more than going through trials and tribulations together, although that is part of it. To share life means that we exchange the nature of who we are with others.

True fellowship with God is intimate, strong, and deep. An exchange of life—an impartation from God—occurs as we have fellowship with God in worship, in prayer, and as we obediently walk with Him in our daily lives. This process is more than a simple exchange of information. God literally imparts His character within us. Through our shared life with God, we participate in His divine nature.

I cannot overemphasize the fact that knowing the will of God is infinitely more than coming to terms with divine information. The will of God is formed within us, and it becomes part of the fabric of who we are! It takes time, and much of what transpires occurs on a level that is deeper than the cognitive level of our understanding. Deep within us, God is building the truth of the eternal Word and the life of the Spirit into the fabric of our souls. He is writing His law on our hearts, and as Ezekiel 11:19 describes, giving us an undivided heart, a new spirit, a heart of flesh in place of a heart of stone.

Intercession Before God

As we meet with God, we can make powerful intercession on behalf of people and situations. This is the place of standing before God, knowing that we belong there, and executing important business for His kingdom. Intercession is not some desperate attempt to talk God into something. Instead, it is the powerful release of spiritual authority to move the heart of God.

The Bible gives us many examples of intercessory prayer:

- Abraham interceded for Sodom and Gomorrah (Gen. 18:22–33).

- Moses interceded for Israel (Exod. 32:11–14).

- David interceded for Jerusalem (2 Sam. 24:17–25).

- A centurion interceded for his servant (Matt. 8:5–13).

- A Canaanite woman interceded for her daughter (Matt. 15:22–28).

- Jesus interceded for Peter (Luke 22:31–32).

- Jesus interceded for His executioners (Luke 23:34).

- Jesus intercedes for us continually (Heb. 7:25).

Intercession is not without cost and it is not superficial. True intercession often involves great anguish of soul and deep suffering of spirit and body. It cannot be done without personal involvement and sacrifice. When Moses interceded for Israel on Mount Sinai, he fully identified with the people for whom he interceded and was willing to share their fate. Could you see yourself mediating before God on behalf of another to the extent that you would be willing to have their punishment cast on you instead of them? Through persevering faith, the saints of God have moved His heart, prayed with authority, engaged in spiritual warfare, and changed the course of human affairs. They continue to do so today!

Moving the heart of God

There is too much fatalism among Christians. Many of us pray, but if we are honest, many will confess that they really believe God is going to do whatever He is going to do and that's that. There are those who secretly believe that prayer is basically an exercise in futility because God already knows what we want before we say it.

What kind of father would relate with his children like that? I would never want my children to say, "Dad's just going to do whatever he wants—it doesn't matter what we say." My wife and I have always had basic desires for our children, and we tried our best to mold their young lives in the ways of respect, love for God and others, personal responsibility, and forward-thinking, productive living. However, we continually adapted our desires for our children to their individual needs and desires. We did not control everything they did, nor try to artificially determine the course of their lives.

We are imperfect parents, but our all-knowing, all-wise God is the perfect Father who has the very best plans and desires for us. His plans are not only designed to prosper us, but also to bring us into complete union with Him. God *does* listen to us, and His plans unfold in the give-and-take of His relationship with us. We can move God's heart the same way any of our children can move ours. But we must not forget that God knows best. God has plans that are beyond our knowledge and understanding. God sees life from a perspective that our limited vision cannot see.

Praying with authority

At times, our prayers are frantic petitions hurled toward the throne of God in anxious hope that something good might happen. However, prayer should be so much more than that. As we meet with God on a regular basis, and as we grow in the depth of our knowledge and experience, our prayers will take on a greater authority. We will not have to feel like a hapless, helpless victim of our circumstances any longer. Instead, the power of God will be exercised through us.

As we commune with God, we will learn that the will of God is more than something we know; it can become part of who we are. As a result, the nature of our thinking will change. Over time, our heart and our perspective will also change. What we feel, think, and do will become more and more reflective of the nature of God. Our prayers will naturally reflect this change of coming more and more into agreement with the will of God.

Have you ever wondered how Jesus could say, "If you ask anything in my name, I will do it" (John 14:14, RSV)? How did He know we wouldn't use that kind of authority for our own lustful desires? It is because He was anticipating the very process we have been talking about. As we become more and more conformed to the will of God, the content of our prayers will reflect it.

It is important to recognize that this is a growth process. Frankly, I am still aware of times when my heart and mind are not aligned with God. My times of meeting with God always reveal when my perspective on a person or situation is not right. Perhaps I have disobeyed God, and the reality of my sin weighs on me. At such times, I have to come to God in humble repentance and stay there day after day until my mind and heart are once again right before God. Then I can begin to pray properly, with the authority and power of God, in accordance with His will.

Engaging in spiritual warfare

The forces that oppose the reign of Christ and the will of God are strong and ruthless. Yet, God has given us both the authority and strategy to combat evil, push back the powers of darkness, and deliver people from sin and its effects. War can be brutal; we should never go looking for a fight. However, we should never cower in fear or give in to the demands of evil. In every situation, victory in battle comes through worship and prayer.

As we engage in spiritual warfare, the real battle is won in the heavenly places—between the wings of the cherubim. Don't go out and hack away with sword and spear, issuing vain threats and silly trash talk against evil. Spiritual warfare requires prudent wisdom. God will always give you two important pieces of information: the strategy of the enemy (what really is going on, not just what seems apparent to the natural eye) and how He wants you to respond.

Second Chronicles 20 gives us a basic pattern for spiritual warfare:

- *The enemy attacks*: The enemy comes against us, against those we love, or against those to whom we are called (v. 1–2).
- *The faithful assemble*: We do not fight the battle alone (v. 3–4).
- *The faithful pray*: We look to God for guidance and deliverance (v. 5–13).

- *The Word of the Lord comes*: The battle is not ours, but God's (v. 14–15).
- *God gives instructions*: He may tell us to flee, or He may tell us to go forward (v. 16–18).
- *God reveals the enemy's strategy*: God gives us insight into what is really happening, even though we cannot see it (v. 16).
- *God assigns positions for the battle*: Where does God want us to be? We must know and remain in our place regardless of the surrounding circumstances (v. 17).
- *God calls His people to stand firm*: We are to stand firm in our faith and in the never-changing promises of our faithful God, refusing to give into fear or anger (v. 17).
- *God directs His people to watch for His deliverance*: We are to keep our eyes and ears open and wait for God to act (v. 17).
- *The people worship*: God has promised victory to us, and we enter into it through worship (v. 18–19).
- *Encouragement is vital*: We will need both encouragement and the reiteration of God's promises to hold the line during the battle (v. 20).
- *Praise leads the way*: We must always praise God, especially when the battle is fierce and it appears that we are losing ground (v. 21).
- *God gives victory*: God will act on our behalf. If we put our trust in the Lord, we will never be put to shame (v. 22–23).

An Open Heaven

In Revelation 4:1, God called to His beloved servant, John, and said, "Come up here!" He wanted to show John things that could only be seen from the perspective of heaven. Today, God calls us to transcend the plane of the natural world, to rise above the mundane–email, voice messages, gas prices, daily responsibilities, sports events, and the news of the day. In the words of Colossians 3:1–2, "Set your minds on things above, not on earthly things." He wants us have our sights set on things above where Christ is, seated at the right hand of God (v. 1).

When we are above the din and cares of the temporal world, we can see things from the perspective of eternity. Life, people, relationships, and priorities appear different from that lofty position. God said that He would meet with us *above* the mercy seat, *over* the ark of the testimony, between the wings of the cherubim—in other words, above the earth and in the spiritual realm. Worship is God's invitation for us to "come up here."

Seeing spiritual realities

As a child, I used to wonder about the universe. I remember being outside at night lying on my back looking up at the stars for hours and wondering where it all ended. It was a wondrous and perplexing thought to consider where, if ever, the universe might reach its outer limit. Time and age have restricted my vision and in many ways dampened my sense of wonder. However, science has made new discoveries that add to my amazement at the vastness of the universe.

Our galaxy alone has billions of stars, and there are billions of galaxies in the known universe. All this is well beyond our ability to comprehend, and we might ask why God would go to such lengths to set us in the midst of such an immense, varied creation. One thing is certain: creation tells us about God. Like all artists, the Creator's identity and nature are indelibly woven into the fabric of all He has created. As Psalm 19:1 declares, "The heavens are telling the glory of God" (RSV). The earth tells of His handiwork. God's creative expression in the world around us is a window into His divine nature.

For example, on a mission endeavor in South America, I was privileged to visit one of the most incredible natural sights I have ever seen—the Iguazu Falls, located on the Parana River at the confluence of Argentina, Brazil, and Paraguay. At the head of the falls, a gigantic horseshoe-shaped panorama hundreds of yards wide, one can don rain gear and walk out on a platform that is completely surrounded by the falls and their mist. As I stood on that platform looking up at the powerful waters falling down toward me and then turning around to gaze at the water rolling away from me, I was reminded of the magnitude of the power of God and the beauty of His creation.

Revelation 1:15 says that the voice of the exalted Christ is "like the sound of rushing waters." At the same moment in which I heard the loud crashing of the water and saw its display of sheer power, I also saw a tiny butterfly, winding its way along the falls, somehow unscathed by the ferocity of the cascading water. It was a precious reminder that God is as powerful as a mighty waterfall, and yet still approachable to the tiny, tender butterfly.

The earth, even with all it amazing wonders, is so very small in contrast to the immensity of the universe. I believe

God created the earth and the universe as He did to show the relationship between the natural order and the size of the spiritual realm. The earth represents what we are able to see, feel, touch, and scientifically verify in the natural realm. The rest of the universe represents what is in the spiritual realm, that which we cannot see with our natural eyes. The point is this: the natural world in which we exist pales in comparison with the spiritual realm. There is so much more that we cannot see.

God invites us to meet with Him in times of worship, to rise above and see a glimpse of the greater reality. This will change the way we see the world and the limited experiential reality of the current age. It was Oliver Wendell Holmes who said that "some people are so heavenly minded that they're no earthly good." It is indeed important that we be effective and fruitful in the flesh-and-blood realities of daily life. However, the greater concern seems to be that we are so often blinded by earthly realities that we have little sense of heaven.

Recognizing an open heaven

Jesus opened the way into heaven. Before His death, a veil—a wall, if you will—separated the place of the people from the presence of God. In the offering of His flesh, the veil was torn in two and the way into heaven was opened (Heb. 10:19–20). Through faith in His Name, we can confidently approach the throne of grace to find strength and help in time of need (Heb. 4:16). Jesus, the pioneer and perfecter of our faith, has gone before us into the Most Holy Place where God dwells and has opened the way for us to enter (Heb. 9:11–12).

The Bible testifies that heaven is also opened in another way at particular times for specific seasons and specific purposes. These are times of divine activity, experiences of divine interaction, windows of opportunity, and showers of God's blessing.

- When Jesus was baptized, the heavens were opened and the Spirit of God descended upon Him like a dove (Matt. 3:16).
- Ezekiel, by the River Kebar, saw the heavens open, and the Word of the Lord came to him (Ezek. 1:1).
- Jacob saw the heavens opened and a ladder that reached to heaven, with angels ascending and descending (Gen. 28:12–13).
- Just before Stephen died, the heavens were opened, and he saw Jesus standing at the right hand of God (Acts 7:55–56).
- The apostle Peter saw the heavens opened, and a great sheet descended to him with all manner of creatures in it (Acts 10:9–16).
- Jesus told Nathaniel that he would see the heavens opened and the angels of God ascending and descending on the Son of Man (John 1:51).
- When God called to John, he saw a door standing open in heaven (Rev. 4:1).

An open heaven is a window of opportunity. Although we cannot see it with our physical eyes, it is a special time when the power of God is ready and available. It is very important that we have spiritual understanding to recognize such times and move with God in the midst of them. It is important to learn to be sensitive to times when the power of God is present to heal, as described in Luke 5:17–26. And we must learn from the failure of the people of Jerusalem, who did not recognize the time of God's visitation to them (Luke 19:41–44).

Recognizing an open heaven is an important part of moving in concert with the will of God. One night, for instance, God directed me to pray for a woman during a prayer service at our church. She and her husband had tried and tried to conceive children with no success. We had prayed for her often and for quite a long period of time, but she was still waiting on God to answer her prayer.

As I was walking toward the altar after praying for someone in the back, I saw this woman praying with a small group. *"Pray for her now,"* God spoke to my heart. I didn't say anything to her or make a general announcement. I didn't even tell her what I was about to do. I simply walked over to where she was, gently placed my hand on her head, and silently asked God to open her womb. That week she called me with the news that she was pregnant with the first of the two beautiful children she would eventually have.

Opening heaven

God loves us and He delights in responding to our prayers. He has also given us divine authority, and we have some say about when the heavens are opened. It is not a "can't miss formula," but we can move God's heart. Here are some things that open heaven:

- the prayer of faith
- pure lives

- unity
- repentance
- worship

The will of God is released in the lives of those who worship in spirit and in truth. We do not have to strive frantically to somehow determine the will of God and hope we hit the mark. Instead, we can be confident that God is building His divine purposes into us and shaping our minds and hearts by His power. God goes before us to make a way for us, opening doors and creating opportunities. We are no longer hapless and helpless, hoping for good fortune. We can function with the spiritual power and authority to move mountains; to speak, act, and pray with authority; and to affect change in people and situations.

Chapter 11

FULFILLING OUR DESTINY

I OFTEN HEAR PEOPLE express their belief that they are being prepared for something. They say that they feel God is getting them ready for something big, but they have no idea what it might be. They consider this big "thing" to be their destiny and seem intent on discovering what it is.

My response to this is that the purpose of our lives is not some grand destiny out there in the future. The will of God—our destiny—emerges and unfolds as we walk with God day by day. While we have an ultimate destination, walking with God is a continuous way of life. The will of God is not a process by which we somehow determine what He is preparing us to do and then going out and doing it. Sure, God may have some major accomplishments for us in the future. However, the point is that *everything we do is big when it is done in the framework of the purposes of God!*

The Promise of Abraham

The first eleven chapters of Genesis—about .009 percent of the Bible—recount many things including the creation of the heavens and earth, plants, birds, fish, animals, and human beings. They tell how rebellion produced a fundamental change in the nature of humanity, creation, and our relationship with God. And they describe how the earth was populated, destroyed by a flood, and then repopulated into diverse languages and cultures. Then in chapter 12, God begins an endeavor which will encompass the rest of the Bible. It begins with one man.

In Genesis 12, God called a man known as Abram—his name eventually became Abraham—to leave his home country and go to a land He would show him. He also made a promise to Abraham and set into motion a plan that spans the ages, all the way to our generation and beyond. God told Abraham:

> I will make you into a great nation and I will bless you; I will make your name great, and you will be a blessing. I will bless those who bless you, and whoever curses you I will curse; and all the peoples on earth will be blessed through you.
>
> —Genesis 12:2–3

This has been referred to as "the promise of Abraham," and it is monumental. When God called Abraham, He certainly called Him to do some things. But more than that, God was calling Abraham to be something. "You will be a blessing." He is not calling Abraham to do something nearly as much as He is calling Abraham to become something. The blessing God has for the nations will in habit Abraham and his offspring. Abraham is being called to be the carrier and the conduit of God's blessing of the nations. Most of us consider our life in God to be something that we do or a message that we convey. Abraham is being called to embody a blessing—to become the blessing.

The Creator of all things has promised that those who walk in the promise of Abraham will be part of a great nation, formed not just to receive a blessing, but to be the vessel through which God will bless *all* people. Abraham was not called to go out and try to bless people. Rather, he was destined to *be* a blessing—to embody and exemplify through his whole life the favor and love of God. This blessing would not only flow *to* Abraham's descendants, it would flow *through* them as well. Through them, God would reach out in love to every family on Earth. Thus, Abraham's children would be a vehicle, a conduit, for the blessing of God for all nations, forever. It flows in to them and through them to all nations, races, tribes, and cultures.

The promise of Abraham flowed down through his biological lineage—specifically through Isaac, Jacob, the sons of Jacob, and, more specifically, through the offspring of Jacob's son Joseph. Later, the promise of blessing flowed through Moses. When it flowed through David, it became infused with royalty and eventually flowed through Jesus.

A change occurred when the promise of Abraham flowed through Jesus. The nature of the promise remained the same, but Jesus changed the way it was transmitted. For centuries, it had flowed through the narrow tunnel of Abraham's natural progeny. However, in Christ it became available to every person on earth. When Jesus came to Earth, He opened the promise of Abraham, not just to those who have Abraham's DNA, but to all who share the faith of Abraham (Rom. 4:16). It is now available to everyone on earth!

Through our faith in Jesus Christ, we become virtual children of Abraham and full heirs of the promise (Gal. 3:29). All the rights and responsibilities of that solemn vow of God from Genesis 12 now apply fully to us. As we enter into faith in Christ, God places us into the flowing current of the promise of Abraham. It is as if God makes that same promise to each of us personally!

Because God has made this promise to us, we are living under its blessing and protection. What's more, our destiny is tied to it. Everything God does for us is a means by which He fulfills it. The will of God for our lives is the unfolding of the promise of Abraham for us and for those we bless. We are blessed so that we may embody a blessing. This is our destiny.

Knowing the Future

The plans of God are developed and released in His time, and His way is opened to us step by step. As we experience an incremental increase in our awareness of God's ways, His will is released in us and through us. His purposes are realized through the work He does within us and the windows of opportunity that are opened before us.

We rarely get a two-day supply of the will of God. I have tried to coerce God into telling me what is ahead, but He won't budge. I have even tried to con God into telling me something, anything, about the future, but it doesn't work. No amount of pleading will persuade God to tell us our whole future. We might receive prophetic glimpses, but most of the time God will only say, "*Today. You have today. The future is Mine. I give you today. Trust Me. I assure you that I am your destination. The end of all things is oneness with Me. I am calling you to Myself and to My heart."*

Jesus tells us not to think about tomorrow but to concentrate on God's will for us today (Matt. 6:34). We can count on the fact that He has our tomorrows in the palm of His hand. Most people vehemently believe that we must determine the course of our destiny and use every means available to try to place ourselves in the best possible situations. They drive themselves crazy in the frenzied use of control, competition and manipulation to position themselves most advantageously. In contrast to this, Proverbs 16:9, one of my favorite Bible verses, teaches us to let the Lord determine our steps.

Daily obedience to the Lord and unwavering trust in the unfolding goodness of His will, frees us from the madness of the world's manipulation and its reliance on "fate." If I honestly did not believe that God holds my tomorrows, I would try to politic and connive my way to a better future, like everyone else. Praise God we do not have to do this, because I believe that ultimately God will place us where He wants us. We must learn to place favor, advancement, promotion, and anything else we desire in the Lord's hands as we do our part and work to the very best of our ability.

The key is that we must choose to be content in whatever state we find ourselves (Phil. 4:11, KJV). We are the Lord's if we are promoted, or if we are not. This does not mean that we should sit idly by and wait for things to happen. When God opens a door, we must walk through it. When God provides opportunities or contacts, we must make the most of them. When God gives us favor, we must use it in the manner for which it is intended.

Genesis 39–41 tells the inspiring story of Joseph, a man who had many special abilities but had been put in prison on false charges. God had great things in store for him, and He had given him a dream and a vision about his future. However, as a prisoner, Joseph had no real idea when, how, or even if it would come to pass. What he didn't realize was that, even while he was in prison, God's plan was unfolding. Even so, Joseph was faithful to God and wisely continued to use the gifts God had given him. When the time came, Joseph was not only freed but also advanced to a high place—the place that God had destined him to occupy.

Even then, Joseph's place of honor and power was not the pinnacle of his destiny; it was a means through which an even greater purpose of God could be realized. As Joseph walked in his destiny, he was part of even greater things: the reconciliation of his own family and the formation and freedom of a nation of people. It would extend well beyond his lifetime. All the while he was in prison, Joseph knew none of this. He had no idea of the great things that God was going to do through him. He was simply faithful to God in the place where he found himself. God did not exalt Joseph simply for the sake of giving him honor, but to put him in a position where he could be part of God's redemption plan.

God's Desire for His Children

John 1:12 promises that when we receive Jesus and believe in His Name, He gives us the power to become children of God. And 1 John 3:2 declares, "Beloved, we are God's children now" (RSV). When we give ourselves to the work of the Spirit and allow Him to lead us, we establish our identity as children of God. We can better understand God's desire for us as His children if we see Him as our heavenly Father.

Jesus, who called God His Father drew the parallel between earthly fathers and our heavenly Father. Therefore, we can understand in some measure God's desire for us as we consider our desire for our own children. If we are good parents, we want certain basic things for our children: that they know they are loved; that they have a strong, healthy sense of who they are; and that they be productive and have respect for others. As parents, we make it our aim to shape our children through love, example, and discipline so that they may become all God has created them to be. We do not want our children be spoiled or to think of themselves as unworthy.

God wants the same things for us. He does not want us be spoiled children who demand the immediate gratification of our every whim. He is not pleased if we believe the world revolves around us and are therefore unable to be self-giving. Neither does He want us to consider ourselves a total failure or a nuisance to Him. Instead, He wants to guide our lives in accordance with His desires. He calls us to walk out His will by giving Him all that we have and all that we are so that we can fulfill His divine purpose.

It is the will of God that we put everything in our lives on the altar of the Lord. When we do this, we are allowing God to do with us as He pleases. He may prosper us or abase us. He may use the things we place on His altar or He may burn them up as a sacrificial offering. He will do whatever gives Him glory. It is our joy as His children to offer ourselves to the Lord in this way and say, "My life is not my own; it is yours. Not my will, but Yours."

A loving father will always do what is best for his child, but this does not mean that he totally ignores what the child wants. Neither does God ignore what we want. Sometimes, the Father will say, "This is what I need you to do." At other times, He may say, "What is it that you really want to do?" God, by His creative design, has made each of us with passions, ideas, abilities, and desires that are unique to us as individuals, and He somehow weaves these gifts into His overall plan for our lives.

As God's children, we are heirs of a very great inheritance. Luke 12:32 says, "It is your Father's good pleasure to give you the kingdom" (RSV). He wants to give us an incredible inheritance beyond our wildest dreams, the kingdom prepared for the faithful from the foundation of the world.

It is important to recognize the great difference between being a hired hand of God and being His son or daughter.

- The hired hand works for a wage, but the child is preparing for an inheritance.
- The hired hand constantly fears that he may be fired. The child knows that the Father's love is eternal.
- The hired hand cares only about the assigned work and its accompanying wage. The child cares not only about the work, but also for the whole farm, which will one day be his.
- The hired hand sleeps in the barn, but the child belongs in the Father's house.

As children of God, we belong in our Father's house. We must stop acting like we don't belong there. We must also stop worrying about messing up and being fired. Instead, we must start thinking and acting like an heir. Let us work hard to show God that we are worthy sons and daughters.

The great miracle of God is that He shares His work with us. God could have done it all without human partnership, but He delights to work with and through men and women. As President John F. Kennedy once said, "Here on earth God's work must truly be our own."[1] The work God gives us is not busywork. He does not intend to patronize us by giving us menial tasks and hoping that we don't mess things up. Rather, the work God gives us is important and vital to the kingdom. No matter how small the task, it is intrinsically tied to the overall divine purposes for the whole earth.

The Divine Game Plan

God is making each of us a new creation, and is changing our desires to conform to His will. As He does this, our goals change from seeking self to honoring Him in our relationships with people. Unholy passions are purged, and God stretches us to do things we would have never chosen to do by our own will. Our abilities are enhanced as we find true purpose by walking in God's destiny.

We all have times when walking out our destiny is painful, discouraging and often arduous. Walking with God is not for sissies, and it will sometimes stretch us beyond our ability to endure. It will test our faith well beyond its limits. But this does not mean it is our destiny to be miserable. Psalm 37:4 promises that if we willingly submit ourselves to the Lord and delight ourselves in His way, He will give us the desires of our hearts. In any situation, we will be blessed as we release our abilities and ideas in service to God.

On a football team, each player's assignment is an important part of the overall scheme of the game plan. Even if a player thinks his part is insignificant, it is vital to the unfolding of each play. If he does not faithfully do his part, the game plan begins to break down and the team looses. The same principle holds when we consider our destiny, the will of God. Each of us has a job to do which affects each other and contributes to God's game plan.

Our destiny is to obey God each day as the divine game plan unfolds. Lives are literally at stake, and we must do what God calls us to do. If we begin to resent a role that seems to be too small, we are of no use to God. If we have to know and approve of the game plan before we willingly decide to participate, we are likewise of no use to God. We choose if we will participate in God's destiny for us. If we have departed from it, we can return to it. We can get back in the game. God needs you and me. The world needs each of us. It is that important!

BIBLIOGRAPHY

The New Interpreter's Bible. Nashville, TN: Abingdon Press, 1998.

The Interpreter's Bible. Nashville, TN: Abingdon Press, 1957.

Strong, James. *The Exhaustive Concordance of the Bible.* Nashville, TN: Abingdon Press, 1980.

Kistemaker, Simon J. *New Testament Commentary.* Grand Rapids, MI: Baker Book House, 1986.

NOTES

Chapter 2
Submitting to the Word of God

1. Martin Luther King, *Strength to Love* (Cleveland, OH: Collins Publishers, 1963).

Chapter 5
Being Led by the Lord

1. E. Stanley Jones, *The Christ of the Mount, a Working Philosophy of Life* (Nashville, TN: Abingdon Press, 1931), 73.

Chapter 7
Receiving Our Inheritance

1. Melvin E. Dieter and Hallie A. Dieter, *Hannah Whitall Smith: God Is Enough* (Grand Rapids, MI: Frances Asbury Press, 1986).

2. William Benke and Le Etta Benke, *Church Wake-Up Call: A Ministries Management Approach that is Purpose-Oriented and Intergenerational in Outreach* (Binghamton, NY: Haworth Press, 2001), 16.

3. William Benke and Le Etta Benke, *The Generation Driven Church* (Cleveland, OH: The Pilgrim Press, 2002), 58.

Chapter 9
Revealed in Worship

1. *United Methodist Book of Worship* (Nashville, TN: The United Methodist Publishing House, 1992), 35.

Chapter 10
Released Through Worship

1. Quote available online at http://quoteopia.com/famous.php?quotesby=oliverwendellholmes (accessed December 2, 2007).

Chapter 11
Fulfilling Our Destiny

1. John F. Kennedy, Presidential Inaugural Address, January 20, 1961, http://www.bartleby.com/124/pres56.html (accessed December 2, 2007).

TO CONTACT THE AUTHOR

Kent Reynolds Ministries, Inc.

P. O. Box 48691

Athens, GA 30604

www.kentreynoldsministries.com